H U S A I N   S A M - T I O   C H U N G

God the Therapist

A True Story of a Man's Search for His Soul

iUniverse, Inc.
Bloomington

iUniverse books may be ordered through booksellers or by contacting:

iUniverse
1663 Liberty Drive
Bloomington, IN 47403
www.iuniverse.com
1-800-Authors (1-800-288-4677)

ISBN: 978-1-4620-0687-8 (sc)
ISBN: 978-1-4620-0691-5 (hc)
ISBN: 978-1-4620-0690-8 (ebook)

Printed in the United States of America

iUniverse rev. date: 06/15/2011

For Muhammad Subuh Sumohadiwidjojo, with deep gratitude.

And, for all my children, Rasyad, Caleb, Rosada, Oriana Rose, Harfijah, Dahlijani, Michael, and Rachman for whom this book was written, so that they might better understand their father's journey.

Acknowledgments

Thanks to my beloved late wife, Harlina Chung, who believed that my story needed to be told and who transcribed this book. I am grateful to one of my oldest friends and my first assistant in the psychodrama theatre of the Human Institute, Sulaiman Dufford, who first edited this book. And a very special thanks to my soul mate Lusijah Rott, who has steadfastly believed that God the Therapist speaks to the needs of the times and has worked devotedly to re-structure and re-edit the entire book for mainstream publication.

Contents

Preface

I recall a time when I was eleven years old in Honolulu, not long after the bombing of Pearl Harbor. Alone in the kitchen, I suddenly burst out crying, punching both of my hips and cursing my physical deformity. I never allowed myself to cry in front of anyone, stoically keeping my true feelings hidden. My seventeen-year-old sister, Helen, who was always secluded in her room reading the Bible, came and gently whispered "Oh Motau (Chinese nickname), why are you so sad? Your leg's hurting bad huh?"

Instantly, I stiffened and stopped crying, fearing to be caught. I wanted to hold her or be held by her, but I pulled back. "No. I'm okay now." I turned to escape.

She delicately put an arm on my shoulders. "You can tell me. I won't say a word to anyone."

Suddenly, it all came out like a flash flood of torrential suffering, babbling tear-filled words tripping over each other, desperately seeking caring acknowledgment of my feelings. The public schools were closed because of the bombing and all the neighborhood boys were excited, saying how they would like to go to war and be heroes and such. I joined in, "Yeah, I wanna be a fighter pilot!"

Everyone suddenly had gone quiet. Then, one after another, "You can't." "How can you?" "They don't let cripples in the Air Force."

I was stunned, my legs wouldn't move. I was just about to hit the kid and go fighting mad as I usually did. An older boy came up, told the kid to shut up, and was about to put his arm on me for support. I turned and limped away with my head held up.

In the kitchen that day, I blurted out to Helen, "I hate my legs, I hate 'em, I hate 'em. They can't run and jump or play football and basketball. They're stupid stumps. Now I can't even be a pilot and help to fight the enemy. Why? Why *me*?" I turned to my sister, "You talk to God all the time, reading God's book, the Bible, so why did God make me a cripple? That's not fair, is it?"

She held both my shoulders, looking me in the eyes, "Listen, Motau, I don't know the answers but I feel strongly God *does* love and care for you, and I think God is testing you, preparing you for a special task, maybe bigger than a fighter pilot. I love you the most of all our brothers. I have watched you and I know in my heart who you are—you are one of His chosen. God has a special gift for your soul. Someday you will see it, because it will be revealed at the right time."

I secretly treasured that moment with my sister and never told anyone. I even hid it from myself, like secretly storing my special marble somewhere so that no one could find it. But in special moments I did remember and I would take it out, rub it and shine it, feel its beauty and secret power, and dream of the moment when I could bring it out and put it to its chosen destiny.

Introduction

Dear Reader,

You are much more extraordinary than you can imagine.

If you are interested in discovering the "light switch" within your self so that you can calm your feelings whenever you feel too anxious, nervous, upset or stressed out, so that your feelings will become calm and peaceful, then you will be interested in reading this book.

If you have difficulty controlling your frustration, anxiety, excitement, irritability, anger, and even rage, then what follows may be of benefit and lasting value.

If you consider yourself an intelligent and basically good person and feel concerned for yourself, for future generations, for your children, and for all of mankind, but have not found satisfactory answers to many of your unanswered questions, you should read on.

If you suspect that there are many truths that personally apply to you, but that these secrets are concealed in parables, fables, and allegorical stories in holy books, old fairy tales, ancient legends and myths that even scholars and priests are unable to unravel. And if you sense that deep within you, these hidden truths are available if you can somehow find the key to unlock them, then what follows will confirm your suspicion and fascinate you as some of these truths are revealed.

If you're embarrassed to say that you are an agnostic or atheist because you have never had a really direct and personal contact with the Power of God, then some of these pages will apply to you.

If you have lost your early enthusiasm and ceased going to church, temple or mosque, but still believe in a Higher Power, then you may be a candidate for miraculous personal and direct contact with the Higher Power that exists within you and without.

If you think you have a soul, but are not sure what it looks like, how mature it is, whether it moves about or understands more than you, and if you truly wish to meet and dialogue with your soul, then be prepared to be surprised as you continue to read.

If you have suspected that somehow there is much more to you than you currently perceive, then you will be pleasantly surprised by what is contained in this writing.

If you have had glimpses of a dormant power deep within your being, you can be assured of its confirmation and continuing presence after reading on.

If you hold the private belief (secret so as not to be laughed at by others) that a good and powerful "Force" from beyond this world has already made its presence known, and you sincerely wish to establish contact with this mysterious Life Force, then by all means turn these pages and your wish may come true.

However, if none of the above applies to you then I would strongly advise that you pass this book on to someone else who may be interested, and you should stop right here. Do not continue reading but simply move on, for idle curiosity can lead to confusion and misfortune when one probes into life's guarded mysteries without genuine sincerity and openness.

---Husain Chung

Outsider

I was born in Shanghai, China, on the 29th of November, 1930, which makes me a horse in Chinese astrology and a Sagittarius in the Western one. At three years of age, I was taken to Hawaii for total hip surgery. My uncles, the two brothers of my father, were M.D.s, and one of them was a staff neurosurgeon at the Shriner's Crippled Children's Hospital. I was admitted there and three and a half years later at age seven, I was discharged, walking without assistance for the first time in heavy leg braces. I then rejoined my family who had moved to Honolulu from Shanghai. I had not seen them during my stay in the hospital and so they appeared almost as strangers after all that time.

From my child's eye, I had been abandoned and exiled from mama, and papa, and country and had been dropped into a strange land of foreign tongues and different ways only to be subjected to four major surgeries, followed by painful rehab exercises from wheelchair to crutches. During the many terrifying dark, lonely, and pain filled nights I had to muffle my screams and crying. I quickly learned that if I got caught for waking the other children in the ward, I was wheeled into a closet for solitary confinement.

With the hospital staff, I put on the face of courage, giving them big smiles and pretending everything was "just fine with me." I worried that if they had nothing to do, if they got bored or saw I was not well, they might decide to try another surgery on me.

Later, after the hospital, facing my peers in the outside world, I assumed that now I would be no different from normal kids. Yet, I felt in the guarded way they watched me, they thought I was not of the same species as they. The sting sank deep when I was bombarded with whispering and stares and finger pointing. Then later came words that stung and burrowed deep into my soft, tender heart—they implanted a huge tick sucking my blood. At first I denied that it originated from them with deliberate

1

intent, or that they knew what they were doing. It was a strange feeling, unfamiliar the first time, but it quickly penetrated to dwell within me as a parasite, an uninvited quest. It was a sensation as if some unknown evil force within had turned me against myself. Much later, I learned its despised name—prejudice.

When I was nineteen years old, I was seeking a higher understanding that would integrate all my questions into some meaningful whole. I was becoming a beatnik weirdo, a mystic seeker of truth. I searched for the intimate dialogues or even diaries of Christ's twelve disciples. I especially wondered how following Christ altered their lives. I would spend many hours in the back stacks of the university's library, totally absorbed in reading old, dusty manuscripts about the secret meetings of the Essenes in their hidden caves, the wandering Hasidic mystics, and the strange whirling Sufis in long robes doing their meditative dancing to fast rhythmic drumming. Twice I had to stay overnight in the stacks because I fell asleep dreaming about slaying demons and didn't hear the last bell before the library closing. But there were no records, no diaries or daily logs of any of those early disciples and followers of prophets and messengers of old. Why?

During my undergraduate years in Missouri, limping around and being the only Chinese student, I felt as though I were an injured soldier unable to find his battalion—I had missed out in the adventures and great battles waged against evil forces by giants and prophets who had once walked upon the earth. Why did I come upon the scene *after* they had all gone, the sword of truth tarnished and broken? Was I born out of a time warp? I was certain they, the giants and prophets, were still alive somewhere, perhaps on some "other side", parallel to this dimension.

As a university student majoring in philosophy and later psychology, feeling totally separate for racial reasons, shunned by the fraternities and other *haoli* students—no matter how hard I tried, I would take late-night walks on and off the campus, sometimes unabashedly crying. I didn't belong anywhere. I was tormented; why couldn't I have been born in the era when human giants and prophets walked upon this earth? I would've been more than grateful to have washed the feet of Jesus or to have been the boy-Friday to disciples Peter or Paul, honored to have carried Muhammad's sword and take care of his camel, or to have been Moses's personal cook, Buddha's private water boy, or even a loyal, hard working slave shepherding Abraham's sheep.

But instead, I actually felt guilt by association for living in this era of man's human injustice, this 20th century with its senseless world wars, merciless genocide and millions of innocent lives lost. I happened to be born a citizen on the side of the conquerors—the grand American experiment of a democratic, cultureless society, the world's mightiest nation that had escalated human injustice with a most heinous push-one-button-no-fail weapon, the atom-splitting bombs of Hiroshima and Nagasaki that contaminated the human gene-pool into future generations, with babies born innocent yet hideously deformed.

In the spring of '54 I was only three weeks from receiving my B.A. degree. I went to the social work class and was the last student to present my paper; the professor asked me to read it aloud.

I began, "I am who I am, and whatever I do is what I am. I am *not* what others see; I am not even what I hope to be. I am simply what I am, with all the strengths and weaknesses and unknown parts of myself. I am all that. If this is what I am, then there must be more to what I could become, which is something I have always felt lies deep within myself, unexplored. I've tried in many ways to get closer with the entity within, but it appears elusive at this time." As I read, I began to feel tremors in my body and tears started coming down my face. I stopped, closed my paper, and simply walked out. I dropped out and began hitchhiking south. It was then that I began the quest for the 'Holy Grail' within. I was planning to find a merchant ship in New Orleans and head for India to find a spiritual teacher, a guru. Since I didn't find a ship in New Orleans that summer, I decided to head to San Francisco to look for a ship to India from there. While in New Orleans, I met Barbara Crandall and she wanted to accompany me. She and I hitchhiked across the country with both of us working as itinerant workers in cotton fields, a short stint as a lumberjack, dishwashers, and many other odd jobs. We were married in Oakland in October. I never did find a ship to India.

A year later, Barbara was pregnant with our first son and I returned to Columbia to finish my B.A. in philosophy. Additionally I picked up my masters in educational psychology and a teaching credential. Then we went back to California with our new son, and I began teaching public school.

Big Sur – My Private Tibet

In June of 1957, I moved my family to the remote southern part of Big Sur, my private Tibetan Himalayas in California. On the advice of my friend Henry Miller, I applied for and was accepted as the sole public school principal and teacher in one of the last little red schoolhouses, with only eighteen children from first through eighth grade.

It was an old building, but comfortable, with live-in teacher's quarters which I used for my lunch breaks, just across from a lovely, secluded beach tucked between two cliffs embracing the Pacific. Sand crabs played hide and seek undisturbed. Life was a Shangri-La, a sanctuary far from the paranoid nuclear threat of the American '50s era.

I was in this beautiful, quiet solitude of Big Sur, one of the last truly untamed, primeval, and magnificently wild parts of America, which resembled certain coastal cliffs of my native land, China. It was here that I quietly practiced various methods of self-development, Gurdjieff prayer, zazen meditation, Tai Chi, fasting on food, going without sex, living in the nude, practicing vows of silence, and reading sacred literature and accounts of the lives of saints and great men. I had no guru or spiritual teacher. I was not a regular user of drugs or alcohol, except for occasional use of marijuana that was plentiful among artists and writers in Big Sur. The nearest police station was in Monterey and in those days, the police didn't come around Big Sur much. It was spooky there, because of metaphysical cobwebs or whatever—candles instead of light bulbs, séances, nudity, and weird hermits living in the woods.

My wife joined me in my interests. We tried everything we knew to disengage ourselves from the habits and inhibitions of our cultural conditioning. In the privacy of our mountain cabin, we were always nude, even when on rare occasions friends dropped in. After living there in Big Sur, we discovered that many creative artists, intellectuals, and individualists practiced and lived as we did. Our isolation was not against life or prejudiced against people, but because we loved life. We sought in our different ways to get in touch with our deeper selves, to evolve further in our reverence for living life's mysteries fully. This was the mindset of Big Sur in the fifties.

All through my early childhood I had felt as though I was living on the other side of reality. This continued the older I became. Barbara and I and our two little boys, Tama (later Rasyad) and Caleb, lived in a cabin two miles directly above the school, with the grand Pacific waves crashing along the cliffs below our living room. We were in an area of tall redwood trees and a small meandering creek that was the source of our drinking and cooking water. Every few weeks, I enjoyed hiking up the creek to clean the debris of fallen leaves and twigs that blocked the screened pipe of our natural mountain water supply. We had no electricity, no telephone, no locks on the door, no radio or TV, not even a daily newspaper. We used a wood stove for cooking and heating the house and kerosene lanterns and candles for light. The deer, squirrels, hawks, coyotes and a fat red fox were the only creatures that came by regularly. Occasionally, lost hunters approached and were given directions, their mouths wide open in disbelief at a nude family in nowheres-ville.

Living in isolation gave me the feeling that I was a law unto myself. I resisted being controlled in any way and I wanted my independence to go in the direction of good for the society at large. I had a cosmic feeling of depression at that time because in pursuing my goal of "Know Thyself", I found the truth to be very depressing. I occasionally smoked marijuana, which gave me a high and took away my pain. Although I recognized an escapist attitude in myself, I did experience some philosophical truths thereby.

One drowsy sunny day I had fallen half asleep when unexpectedly, I had a vision of a room filled with people. They appeared to be a cross-section of people of various races, ages, and economic strata. I was in their midst. In fact I felt quite at home, that this was where I belonged. I sat up and pondered the meaning of this vision.

The Unexpected Guest (Or Angel?)

Among the residents of Big Sur, it was customary to send interesting hitchhikers to each other's homes as short-term guests. One day a young man named Jerry, wearing torn jeans, sandals, and hair down to his shoulders, arrived and requested shelter for a night or two. I invited him into our cabin. After his initial embarrassment at finding us casually in the nude, Jerry joined us by undressing. He was about twenty-four, twenty six, around my age. I think he was Jewish, although I was not certain. He was one of the hippy beatniks, and he happily shared ingredients from his knapsack to make a dynamite curry for us.

We talked about Gurdjieff, whom he had never heard of. I gave him a good talk about my life of spiritual quest and he asked where he could purchase books about Gurdjieff. I told him I imagined in a big city, perhaps like San Francisco.

I said, "If you can find such books, I'd like you to buy the Maurice Nicole book and I'll repay you."

"Yah, I will," he said as he wrote out a book list. "I also want to find spiritual enlightenment. I'll be on my way to San Francisco tomorrow." He asked me what I had concluded from all that I had read, what I was looking for, and how he would know if he found something I would be interested in.

I said, "In your travels, if you should come upon a group of people who are into some spiritual study, you can let me know. But if the people all wear the same kind of clothing, then I would not be interested, because they would be a kind of cult. I would be interested in a group with normal people who come from all walks of life with no distinguishing dress or behavior. The group would appeal to a broad spectrum of people with different lifestyles and from different stations of life."

"That's interesting," he said dubiously. "I don't know if there is such a group. Groups usually have a certain similar identity."

6

"Well, anyway, if you find a Maurice Nicole book, send me a copy."

After we finished his delicious curry, he asked me if I wanted to try some peyote. I said sure. That was my first experience with peyote. He proceeded to peel the peyote buttons, crack them like little nuts, and then peel the fuzz. We started chewing them. I ate maybe ten or twelve buttons.

"How long before it takes effect?" I asked.

"About forty-five minutes," he answered.

So I waited and waited. Gradually, I started feeling a buzz, like the sound of bees all around me. "Is that the sound of the universe, or just my own head? Do you hear it too?"

"Yeah," he said. "I hear it. I always get that buzz. It really sounds like your head is in the middle of a hornet's nest." And that buzz just went on and on and on.

Pretty soon we wandered off to the back porch from where we could look out and see the ocean below, all the way up the coast to the lighthouse. We watched the hypnotic flashing light through the light mist. There was a full moon. We stood there, looking at the moon, and I said, "Do you see those rings around the moon?"

"Where? Around the moon?"

"Yeah. You see it too?" I counted the rings, all those concentric circles. There were seven, including the moon itself.

That peyote experience seemed to confirm that what I was looking for did exist. I could feel an inner entity arising in me much more powerfully; I became more aware of its vibration. I remember taking notes, but later on I couldn't even read them! I think it lasted for about six or seven hours —a good long time, this experience.

The young man left mid-February 1958 and ten days later he sent me a postcard from San Francisco, which said, "I think I've found the group. I'll come by and see you."

I remember before I met this young man, having written a kind of summary of my thoughts, discoveries, and the conclusions of all my knowledge and experiences of life—what I knew and what I didn't know and what I suspected to be true but had not confirmed by experience. One of the things I wrote was that there is an unknown source of energy, understanding, and wisdom within myself and in all people, but it is largely dormant. I could not reach it no matter what I did. I only had fleeting glimpses of it now and then, but knew it was definitely there. I was trying to break through the barriers to reach it and was frustrated because I couldn't seem to do it. I had given up hope of going to India or anywhere else. I no longer felt this was the way to go—through a great teacher. I knew that I wasn't able to read minds at will, with a Buck Rogers X-ray mind. Now and then I could get a glimpse if I concentrated on what someone was feeling or thinking, but I knew I couldn't just zap right into it.

I knew I had a potential, but couldn't really get to it. I couldn't talk to trees, or birds or animals. But I felt those things were possible. I had read the Bible, the New Testament, the Qur'an, the Baghavad Gita, Socrates, and others; I knew there was a presence of the greater good in all of us, but it took great discipline to put it into practice. No matter what I tried to do, I would forget, or waiver and that continually frustrated me. I felt it was almost impossible to be a good man, much less a great human being. It seemed easier to be a son of a bitch or a lazy bastard. But I was also not interested in being a saint.

By then, most of the ideas in my head were from intellectual readings, and although I had had a number of human experiences, I still felt myself influenced by other thinkers. When the great thinkers got "their thing", they got a gift. Why couldn't I receive that kind of gift? I felt unjustly treated. I believed that there is a cave, protected by dragons like in some old myth, and behind and beneath this cave or in the back there would be a golden treasure that exists in all of us. And once one could get into the room, past the bogeymen and slaying of those dragons, we would all—not just the gifted few—be wealthy in the spiritual sense.

So whoever rules the heavens, this god must have set these traps. *Why is he setting these traps?* I felt I was one big trap myself. My mind would trip me up. My emotions would trip me up. My sloth. My inability to be persistent and determined. My will was giving out. I was ready to leave Big Sur. It just wasn't happening. The hermit life, voluntarily being a monk wasn't getting me anywhere. The peyote did kind of open me up, giving me a glimpse that such spirituality exists. But then, after the peyote experience, it was worse. I really had the blues, or the blahs. My deepest prayers went unanswered.

So in March 1958, that was where I was—stuck—when this kid came back. We had a long talk. He was a bit nervous and seemed a little guilty, a little uncomfortable. I asked him what had happened.

"Well, I found this bookstore in San Francisco. It's called The George Fields Bookstore. It specializes in mysticism and the occult, and all the books on my list were there, every book including Gurdjieff. There was a whole section on Gurdjieff and Ouspenski, and Maurice Nicole—all the volumes of Maurice Nicole were there," he said.

"Oh, really." I said.

"Yeah, and that's not all. I was standing there looking at these books. I pulled out a Maurice Nicole book and was glancing at it, and this old man in his sixties, with a funny hat, came and stood by my side." Apparently it was the owner, George Fields himself. "And he saw me reading the book and said, 'Oh. You're interested in Gurdjieff. Are you a Gurdjieff student?' I said no, but that I had been told it might be an interesting method. So he said, 'Well, if you're interested in Gurdjieff, there's a meeting being held tonight by one of his disciples. If you'd like to come, it's at 8:30.' So I said yes, and the old man wrote down the address and time for me. And I went to the meeting."

The bearded young man with hair down to his shoulders walked into the meeting and sat in the back row. He looked around, noticing there were some well-to-do businessmen, some ordinary working people, some office people, and a couple of people like himself sitting in the meeting room.

"We were all waiting," he continued, "and then a tall lanky British man in his mid-fifties came up on the stage and walked to the lectern. We all watched as the man stood there, closed his eyes, and took some deep breaths. I noticed other people closing their eyes. The British gentleman stood there at the lectern as if preparing himself before beginning his talk. It seemed like a long time that the British gentleman stood there with his eyes closed, not saying or doing anything. Then he finally started speaking. He introduced himself as John G. Bennett and started talking about his experience. He was a good speaker."

"What did he speak about?" I asked the kid.

He got a little embarrassed and upset, and said, "I don't know."

"What do you mean, you don't know? How long were you there?"

"Over an hour." He replied.

"So what happened?" I asked.

"I fell asleep."

"You what?" I blurted.

"I totally bombed out. I don't know what happened. I bombed out."

"Then what happened?"

"Well, I opened my eyes and the whole room was empty. So I got up and looked around, and noticed on one end of the room, there were all these women's shoes by one door, and on the other end of the room, all these men's shoes next to another door. And the tall Englishman came to me and asked me would I like to join them. I said, no, not right now, and I split."

"*You what*? You didn't find out what they were doing in those rooms?"

"No, I thought I'd come and let you know about it."

"So when are they meeting again?" I asked.

While Jerry was telling me all this, I could not help noticing my body's instant reaction, as if the black void emitted a loud scream. An inner fear and excitement come from my depths. A strong vibration I had never felt before flash-flooded throughout my entire body as if drawn by a powerful magnetic force, by-passing my skeptical mind.

Before I was fully conscious, I heard my own voice blurt out, "*That's it!*"

Jerry left shortly after that. The last I heard, he had gotten an inheritance and was on his way to Greece. Later, I could not help but wonder if Jerry was in reality an angel in disguise so that I would not flip-out in encountering a real angelic being.

The George Field's Book Store

I didn't know what it would be like. Before that young man came to visit, I had felt and written that once I was able to get in touch with the entity within myself, my whole life would drastically change—and that such an enlightenment would drastically change me. It would be a miracle of sorts. Up until then, I hadn't experienced anything like that in my life. If there had been changes in me, it was me making the changes consciously. These were changes brought about by my own actions, not changes that came from outside myself.

The kid had given me the bookstore address off the receipt for the book that he had purchased. The Maurice Nicole book had been very expensive, so instead of buying that one, he had bought Ouspenski's "In Search of the Miraculous".

It was a Wednesday night. He told me that the meetings, these lectures, were on Tuesday and Thursday nights. So tomorrow night, it would be the same time and the same place. He also said he believed I would need an invitation.

The next day, I dismissed my students early, packed the family in our old, dirty, pine-cone-debris Ford station wagon, and sped north. The leaky radiator left a steaming white cloud along the treacherous zig-zagging Highway One up the Big Sur coast for the next hundred fifty miles to San Francisco. The two boys loved the exhilaration of dad's wild drives, but not my petrified wife.

It was a chilly, windy evening when we arrived in San Francisco. We looked in a phone book for The George Fields Bookstore and found it was near Polk and California. It was rush hour and there were no parking spaces out front, so I double-parked and my wife stayed in the car with the two boys.

I went into the bookstore and looked around for the Gurdjieff section. I found it and took a book out, pretending to read while looking around out of the corner of my eye at the whole place. I saw an old man with a funny hat talking to an elderly woman. I wanted to get his attention and get an invitation to this meeting, as the kid had done.

I was standing there waiting, waiting, waiting, and the guy was still talking to his customer. I thought maybe he just didn't notice me. Here I was, standing next to the bookshelf like the kid had done, but this old man with the hat didn't seem to see me. So I began to kind of like, "Ommmmm," trying to put out a strong vibration. I looked at him again, but he didn't pay any attention to me. I thought maybe I wasn't spiritually enlightened enough, so I straightened myself out, and tried again, "Ommmm."

Then I realized I had opened the wrong book. It wasn't even a Gurdjieff book. So I put that book back and reached for Maurice Nicole. I got one of those down and went through the same thing, but he still didn't pay any attention. I wondered how come it had worked for the kid and not me?

Finally, I couldn't wait anymore, so I walked up to him. I was going to politely interrupt, but he said, "I beg your pardon. Can't you see I'm talking to a customer? Will you please wait?" He was polite, but firm. So I waited and waited, and finally I thought, *my God, my wife will get a ticket for being double-parked.*

Finally the customer left and I said, "Well, I'm interested in Gurdjieff." And I just stood there looking at him. Remember, Gurdjieff was a secret society.

He paused and then said, "Yes?" I thought, *well, what's he talking about, 'Yes?' Wasn't I good enough for it?*

I said, "I have studied a great deal about Gurdjieff and I know Maurice Nicole and most of his books." And I paused, looking intently into his eyes, waiting for his reaction.

He stood there looking at me for a minute and then he said, "Well, are you interested in buying more books?"

"No." I said. The pauses were very pregnant.

"Well, then, how can I help you?"

By this time I was getting really upset. I thought I was using my best spiritual demeanor, whatever that meant. Finally it was just intolerable for me and I blurted out, with as much dignity as possible, "I understand there's a meeting tonight with a visiting lecturer and I'd like to get the time and the address, so I can attend."

He frowned and said, "Who told you that?" I told him about this friend of mine, the kid, and he said, "Oh, that young man. Well, I suppose

I could if you're interested." So he wrote down the address and I thanked him and split. I jumped in the car and we took off.

I started driving like a maniac, certain that I could find the place by instinct, following a vibration or something. We wound up in the northern part of San Francisco, still looking and looking. Then we realized that we had to go all the way back, because the meeting place was only a block from the George Fields Bookstore right there on California Street. The lecture was being held in the Arthur Murray Dance Studio and there was no parking except for a yellow zone.

Once again my wife sat in the car with the kids while I ran upstairs to check it out, because I liked to check things out before introducing my whole family to it. And here is what happened in that room upstairs.

Mr. Bennett explained about a new spiritual group called Subud that he had become aware of in Coombe Springs (the international Gurdjieff center). He said that he had felt for some time that although the Gurdjieff exercises were helping others, they had no longer been helping him. Upon hearing about the spiritual exercise of Subud, he had decided to try it for himself. Subud came out of Indonesia and the spiritual exercise was called latihan, the Indonesia name for exercise. Mr. Bennett said the latihan experience was the soul's contact with the power of God. After doing the latihan for two and a half years, he felt he must share this new spiritual exercise with his Gurdjieff students in Coombe Springs and elsewhere. He said words couldn't explain the latihan and that to really understand it, one must experience it. After a few introductory words about relaxing and surrendering, Mr. Bennett said, "Begin".

So I closed my eyes and tried to relax. I knew that surrendering meant to just take a deep breath, relax, and let go of my will power in order to follow whatever happens. I thought, *I'm a free-thinking Bohemian, so this should be a snap.*

My breathing was normal and nothing unusual happened for about a minute, except for the quiet stillness in the room full of other standing men. I could feel my body relaxing, and without my thinking about it, my body began to sway slightly. I made no effort to stop its slight swaying motion. I could sense an inner vibration in my midsection like the first trembling before an earthquake.

Then it happened.

A rumbling began in the pit of my stomach. From a mild trembling, the vibration increased into a kind of petit mal seizure, something approximately equivalent to a Richter 4.0 quake. Suddenly my legs buckled and before I realized it, my body had collapsed and I had fallen on my knees onto the hardwood floor.

Now my eyes popped open, and I was looking in the mirror. I saw all these men behind me, still standing in perfect rows, some of them seeming to be praying, or going "Ommmmm" quietly. I saw myself kneeling on the floor with eyes wide open.

The dance hall was floor-to-ceiling with mirrors. I saw Mr. Bennett hopping about like a kangaroo between the rows of men. I thought, *how strange....* Embarrassed that I was the only one on the floor, I quickly stood up. The thought crossed my mind that I must be the least spiritual of this whole bloody quiet group—just like the class fool throughout my school years, the ugly class cripple the *pa-ke* (Hawaiian for Chinese) who walks funny. That sinking *deja vu* childhood shame feeling that I hadn't felt for years, returned.

Well, so what? Screw them. I am what I am. How others see and judge me is a projection of their own crap. They can shove it or stuff it in their pipe and smoke it. I stood up and closed my eyes again, determined to let whatever might happen take it's own course without my interference. Letting go of my will power to control and manipulate was, for me, a feeling of helplessness. I took a deep breath and just let everything go.

Although I was fully aware, I again felt that recurring vibration within, causing me to sway, and the same trembling sensation as if I were a musical pitchfork. I noted the more I let go (like exhaling), the more the tingling vibration moved throughout my entire body. I relaxed deeper and then all the way, letting myself surrender and trusting my life to this strange, unknown force. I said to myself, "Well, the hell with it. If I have to start from the bottom, then I must be the lowest, so here goes."

Again, it happened on its own. This time the vibration jumped to Richter 6.0. My knees kissed the floor, but this time as if in stop-frame slow motion. My knees trembled, slowly buckling as though I had been tripped by that bully on my first day in grade school in front of the whole class. My classmate's laughter and giggling had made my ears swell red as I struggled to stand up, pushing on my new clumsy steel braces and heavy boots, slipping and falling again flat on the floor. From that moment on, I had hated school.

Then, I realized my mind had better not get hung up in self-analysis, because the action seemed to slow down. So I took a still deeper breath and really let go of my thoughts. This time I really didn't care what my mind or anybody else thought.

Unexpectedly, as I went deeper into this latihan contact, up surfaced all the past buried stores of burning rage, hurt, confusing injustice, and other people's cold indifference, exposing all my twenty eight years of feeling abandoned, neglected and rejected—images of the cast-away cripple, the terrible racial prejudice, ugly hates spilling out for all the world to see.

The desperate part of me that desired and needed to understand the meaning of it all was the hardest for me to ignore and let go, but ultimately I did. I was able to simply accept that I could not comprehend that this contact was bringing out my tortured past as if I were on somebody's therapeutic couch. I thought if I'm not ready for the great spiritual revelations yet, then I'll take my chances and simply trust the moment.

Pain and suffering had been my closest companions for years, so if letting go meant letting all that hurt come out, then damn the consequences. This seemed like a big risk, because whenever I had let go of my rage in the past, I always ended up in fights and was soon sent to see the principal or boss, who either punished me or fired me, as the case may have been. So I ended up punished, fired, and/or isolated even more.

I continued letting go in the latihan, letting go of everything; my stubborn will, heart and feelings, my pet hates and likes. I let it all go. Even my fears and skepticism and all my *whys*—I let them go. Wanting to analyze was the most difficult thing for me to let go of in the early latihans. It did not even matter if God existed or not—that was His self-identity problem, not mine! I had enough of my own baggage of junk to deal with.

I had no idea what the others in the room were experiencing. I was only aware of what I was going through. I knew this was an unknown powerful force coming from a higher source. I was not imagining it and I was not doing anything to cause it. There was no guru or leader influencing or telling me what to do, just a bunch of people with their eyes closed in a semi-lit room. I thought if this is the price for admission, I will pay; let's get the show of enlightened revelation started.

I found my body rolling on the floor. It was like being tossed by the huge waves on Waikiki Beach as a young boy learning body surfing. I let myself go with the monstrous, rolling, turbulent white foam lifting my helpless tiny body like a pebble in her large ocean *kahuna* arms. Below, I could see the white sand on the ocean bottom as the back current was sucked up into the white, hungry, curling mountain of foaming white wave. As my head went straight down in a kamikaze dive, I bent over and fell rolling on the sea bottom, tumbling like a helpless rolling stone.

On the polished hardwood floor, I went prostrate on my knees, my hands covering my face, forehead touching the ground. I began swaying from side to side, then rocking forward and backward on my knees, then slowly in circular motion. In the same kneeling position, a trembling, rumbling quake resurfaced from deep down. Then quick, short gasping breaths, choking, and then—space collapsed and time left me in a swirling void. My early life began flashing back like a film in reverse, and many of my early childhood traumas began spontaneously coming to the surface.

I am a happy, laughing three-year-old boy playing with my Amah's big breasts. She is giggling. There is no pain, no want, and the world is a safe and happy place. Then I hear whisperings in another bedroom. Is that mama crying?

More whisperings in the house. Why is mama crying? My brothers and other boys are playing and laughing outside. But I cannot join them. I am always held and carried by Amah, who will not let me get away.

Suddenly, I am pulled away from my Amah. She struggles, holding me tighter. Everyone is upset, screaming, and crying. Amah is waving at me, with big teardrops on her cheeks. I am in total confusion, not knowing what is happening. I am torn apart. There is a big explosion. My heart flies out and cracks into a thousand pieces.

This had been my first real encounter with the incredible power of suffering and its devastating impact. It was the first introduction to my life long companions—chronic pain and suffering.

The latihan slowly ended on its own, just before I heard Bennett say, "Finish." I opened my eyes. Bennett was standing next to me. I was flat on my stomach with both arms and legs spread-eagled. All the others had finished earlier and left the room.

What had seemed like hours ago, when the latihan first began, was actually less than an hour. I was gratefully relieved that no one had disturbed me. When I stood up, I saw a pool of tears, evidence of my forgotten childhood revisited.

Mr. Bennett asked, "Powerful, isn't it?"

I said, "I don't know what I felt, but yes, it was strong. I think it was ridiculous, what I was doing."

"No, no, no. Just keep it up. Just keep following spontaneously whatever moves you." So he made me feel a little better, that maybe it was all right, whatever I was doing. I felt a little apologetic for no reason. I was in another space. I thought I was exhausted, or something. Bennett leaned over, talking to me with such kind patience, and said, "We'll be doing this twice a week here. Do you have any questions?"

"Can I do this by myself?" And then I asked, "Can I turn others on to this?"

He replied, "Oh, yes, most definitely. It is between you and God. For now, we do latihan twice a week here, and I hope to see you again."

"Okay."

I reflected, how can anyone with any common sense believe what I had just experienced? Before my opening to the latihan, no one even asked me what I believed or what my doubts were or what I had expected of this spiritual exercise.

There were no prayers, no hallelujahs, no amens, no hands touching and blessing my head. No one paid any attention to others or engaged in any social interaction. Surprising, and what a relief this was! There was no leader or authority present; each man was on his own, doing his own thing, but in a group setting. As I was leaving, no one stared at me or asked me why I was crying or what I had been doing on the floor.

Afterwards, I had no ill effects, no fuzzy or upset feelings. I was actually very clear-headed and relaxed. I went outside, got in the car, and told Barbara about it. She was a little skeptical and a little fearful. I asked her if she wanted to attend, but she did not think so right then. I decided to return again the next week.

By that time it was almost eleven or twelve o'clock at night. We went out to eat, then in silence, we left San Francisco. Reflected in the rear view mirror were romantic city lights flickering on rolling hills, and the city's sentinel, the Golden Gate Bridge, with its yellow lights blinking lover's farewells through the low-hanging mystic fog. We headed quietly south, back to our home in Big Sur, Tibet. The Pacific waves crashed as if kissing and caressing the pain and tears off the rocky cliff, an ancient, jagged-scar face of many tragic human sufferings. The moon lady, in her long, white-spread transparent nightgown, glistened silver and softly kissed and caressed her Pacific *kahuna's* huge, heaving, wet, sensuous, night-jade body. Somewhere, a baby sea lion's whimper echoed as she turned in her sleep, snuggling closer into the warm, safe folds of the giant sonorous sleeping mother below the cliff's edge of the great American continent.

As we turned into the narrow, curving, dirt path up the hill towards our small, tucked-away cabin, the giant 2000-year-old fragrant redwood trees swayed and bowed in reverence and gratitude to the great powers of their earth mother's creation, in total harmony with the night wind's song of soothing surrender.

I have never experienced or seen God, but to my utter amazement, I felt as though a heavenly perfumed breath had engulfed my entire world—somehow like a thief in the night, it entered the dark void deep within my being and released that child-mute from its years of bondage. I was overwhelmed with deep gratitude.

My head on the steering wheel, I wept again in gratitude, feeling truly forgiven, as Barbara carried our two sleeping sons, Tama and Caleb, into our warm safe home. I could hear my voice muttering, "Oh God, God, God." More crying…

I felt I was saying good-bye to all the spirits of my past, and saying hello to my real Father as I was finally embraced and welcomed back home with love, from whence I had long ago left and gotten lost. Now He found me instead. For the first time in my entire life, I did not feel like a stranger in a hostile, alien world. I was home on the other side, where souls are born. *I will never, never leave again*, I vowed to myself.

Again and again the tears kept flowing until I fell asleep on the steering wheel. When I woke, the full moon was high above, and next to me was a steaming hot cup of tea that Barbara must have brought. The house was cozy and sleepy when I went in. The next day I returned to my job as the sole teacher-principal of the one-room red schoolhouse at the southern end of Big Sur.

Getting Out of the Way

During the hundreds of subsequent latihans, I was always conscious throughout. I trusted that even though I did not fully understand the meaning of these experiences, they were something I badly needed.

Fully conscious, I noted that my awareness always remained as an objective witness, a nonjudgmental bystander, and I was both the outsider and the person within experiencing the goings-on. But if I tried to think and figure out the meaning of my sounds and movements, the action would automatically stop. If I didn't think about it or try to understand the meaning, then the action would continue. Yet, I could stop it at any time. At no time did I ever feel faint or go unconscious.

No one was influencing me—all I needed to do was stand quietly, close my eyes, and either say "begin" to myself or just relax and let go. If I even thought of stopping it, it did instantly. I found I could do this anyplace and anytime I chose. I found that late at night or around dawn, the action was much deeper or more subtle and fine.

In subsequent latihans, I was aware of my body crawling and leaping like various wild animals, making strange animal sounds and movements. It was sometimes so loud in our cabin that my terrified wife would speed down the narrow dirt road with our two boys in their little red wagon.

After such wild activity, I would fall dripping wet and exhausted. I had absolutely no idea why I was behaving in such a strange manner. In the end, after all manner of "stuff" was lifted and cleaned out, I felt tired but refreshed and rejuvenated. Afterthoughts occurred to me. From all I had heard, read, or known of other's experience of salvation enlightenment, "satori", or being "born again", such experiences were usually accompanied by indescribable bliss, ecstasy, great peace, understanding, brilliant light, visions of heaven, a loving hand from above reaching down and lifting one upward into compassionate embrace, and other wonderful experiences. Maybe this really did happen to others. But my latihan experiences did not even come close to resembling this type of instant salvation. Instead I experienced recurring old wounds, old karmas, buried hurts—a total restructuring of my past life experiences.

Childhood Skeletons

The images from childhood traumas continued pouring out in latihan. I was revisiting memories seared deeply into my being that I was no longer even conscious of.

I am dressed in my starched pressed shorts, stiff white-collared shirt, and a stupid hat that uniformed private students wore in the Christian Missionary schools of China before communism.

My mother and I emerge from a large shopping building with giant Indian Sikhs as security guards. The guards swing their long hard clubs, cracking the heads and bodies of beggars to make space for us, the more fortunate, to enter our black British limousine. The streets near the door are packed with beggars, pleading with dirty hands extended.

We enter the limo. I reach in the little short-pants pocket of my sailor outfit and pull out my school lunch money to give to the beggar woman. Instantly, the ragged mother with a screaming infant on her half-naked breast leaps on the running board and sticks her hand through the open window. I quickly give her the money. Just then, Mama or the chauffeur quickly rolls up the back window and we speed off. The beggar's hand is caught in the window, her clenched fist still holding the money. The screams and shouts are muffled within the enclosed limo as the woman falls and is dragged until the window is rolled back down. I turn back and see her still holding her crying infant, rolling on the filthy street. Sweaty, half-naked rickshaw coolies and the crowd of beggars wave their fists angrily at us, cursing us, as the chauffeur guides the silent limo into our high-gated estate.

The air is now thick and black with smoke from crashing, exploding bombs, falling, crashing buildings, torn streets, and those eerie ear-piercing frantic drums I've heard and seen in the Chinese operas. Everyone is wearing ugly, scary monster masks like at mardi gras, but no one is laughing here. Long guns with sharp knives are poking and jabbing at the screaming crowd, puncturing and drawing blood from baby's eyes, faces, and bodies, like cattle being prodded toward their imminent slaughter. Those with the rifles and swords, the hated Japanese, the merciless enemy, are a race similar to myself, but then the images alter. Now they are white men in uniforms, and then change again to ferocious dark Mongols on wild, stampeding horses, wearing animal fur hats and long robes, yelling and shouting commands I can't comprehend.

I re-experienced the time when I left home from Hawaii at eighteen to begin my university studies. The latihan room felt heavy as if a dark overcast cloud pushed me down to the floor, returning me to my second year at the university. At that time I was carrying so many unanswered questions as a philosophy major. All these questions, for which I had no answers, I put in a special locked box I created. This was my "secret box of ambiguities" or perplexing conundrums, to which some day I hoped the answers would come. Eventually this locked box of secrets quickly overfilled with more puzzling concerns, such as strange anomalies and contradictions, kabalistic cryptograms and sacred parables, esoteric axioms beyond known paradigms, and other obsessively puzzling issues causing me great stress now in latihan. I felt as if a grand mal seizure attack was coming.

The latihan was in full gear, and the world suddenly exploded under me.

A dark anger and blind hate blasts like a fiery volcano. I spew obscenities at the top of my voice in that room. Never since childhood have I experienced such incredible rage. It even shocks and terrifies me. I pound the floor, throw my body against the wall, beat my head and body with my clenched fists. I scream and rage at everything imaginable, like a chained Prometheus. I feel my guts ripped wide open and my innards torn and chewed by ugly vultures, feeding madly as I squirm and struggle to get them off. But the more I struggle, the more intolerable the agony becomes.

Finally, my body falls in total exhaustion from high jagged cliffs, hitting and further tearing my flesh as I plunge and crash against the rocks below. The waves crash and wash my bleeding, twisted limbs. I can hear the seagulls squawking, circling the bleeding pile of flesh on the smooth, wet boulder. I can feel the salt water and white foam mingling with my tears. I feel my heart being torn and ripped into thousands of tiny little pieces of dark black morsels similar to the chopped liver I'd often seen the servant cook in China in our Shanghai home. I can't tell if I have died or dreamt that I have died.

A horrible stillness comes, the stillness of the dead, the air frozen in deafening silence as if the world has died, and I can't unpop my stuffed eardrums. This quietness terrifies me more than chaos, for I know the worst is still to come.

My head goes groggy, eyes blurry, mouth dry, and all sensation leaves my body. I know that soon the great evil kahuna beast and his assistants will come to torture me again and again without respite.

My body is now strapped tightly down on a cold steel slab. A large blinding light brighter than Jupiter is lowered closer and closer until the white light envelops me entirely. A circle of strange aliens covered in long white gowns with round, blue and black eyes, are peering over their white masks, small shining metal pencils, tongs and forks in their hands, huddled around me. Am I their dinner? Ghastly long needles for sick horses dance and wave above my clouded vision. My heart stops.

In that dark cavern I hear and feel a deep growling snore vibrating the ground beneath me, the Beast's warm foul breath, so close that my hair moves. My naked skin begins to quiver as if being pricked by that old, smelly, turtle-faced acupuncture doctor who was often called whenever one of us was ill in Shanghai. I know I am in the filthy home of the evil kahuna who has been expecting me. My small hands slowly grope, feeling for something to grab, but for what I cannot even think. I feel round, splintered bones encrusted with rotting flesh and quickly let go. I open my mouth to scream for help, but no sounds came forth.

And then it all becomes even more intense. At first slowly, then faster, a wall of rushing water tears from my legs below, swirls around my hips, twists my guts, and sledge-hammers my chest, triggering my heart to beat violently like a thunderous blast imploding in my head with such force that I spin in agonizing pain. I feel brain tissue bursting out from my ears, nostrils and eye sockets, oozing all over like long, slimy worms. The horrendous pain recedes back down my legs, and before I can catch my breath, it zooms up again like an undercurrent, bouncing off the cerebral walls like sharp splintered, glass, twisting and splitting with such violence that it blows out the flickering flame of my infant awareness. I open my mouth, but no sounds come forth.

I am held down by a heavy weight. Unable to move, I raise my head and see only a white, hard landscape from my chest down. I am in a fresh, chalky-smelling cast with only tiny toes sticking out at the end not knowing who they *belong to. I turn and see a little guy named Butterfly with both hands held up as if in a stick-up robbery. Both hands have fingers spread and tied with gut strings to the rim of what appears to be a tennis racket.*

I somehow know that he was severely burned, toasted in a fire, and that both his parents had died in their burning home. Only he survived. Butterfly whispers nervously, but I can't understand a word. There are many strange children in that ward of thirty other aliens, some without arms, missing legs, blind or limping with crutches. I cannot see or recognize anything familiar.

Have I somehow landed on the planet of the cripples? Again, Butterfly is mimicking and gesturing. With both feet, he holds his pillow over his face, biting it. Only the far-off lamp on the night attendant's desk glows in the dimly-lit ward, making shadows on the far wall, grotesque twisting bars, bed posts and pulleys, suspending white casts with legs in the air.

A group of cripples crowds and crams their necks to peer through a small window above a shining steel door. Huffing, puffing, groaning sounds can be heard behind the door. The nightgown-clad kids giggle with hands to their mouths. Suddenly, the crowd scatters and leaps to their beds, hiding under the sheets, pretending to sleep. The night nurse emerges, fussing with her half-opened white uniform. Following her is the night security watchman.

Again, I feel the rumbling recurring from below, the same rushing wall of pain rising upward—I can hear my voice this time, screaming for help to stop the evil beast before I am mauled to pieces. I see the night nurse, her face twisted in an ugly threat, yelling and running towards me. Butterfly frantically signals with his mouth biting his pillow. I imitate him. I pull the pillow on my face and bite hard. I can hear her, "I warned you again to stop crying and screaming. You're waking everyone up, damn you! You are going into the back room again, but this time for the rest of the night!"

The other kids are terrified and plead with her not to. She tells them to shut up, or else they, too, will go. Butterfly has tears in his eyes, staring in horror at me. She pushes my prison-barred cage, the crib, and we rush out of the ward into the dark back room, with only a tiny window facing giant palm trees whose shadows flicker on the room's walls like menacing ghosts.

I hear my own screams as the cage-on-wheels is pushed into the dark room and the huge door slammed. The shadows on the wall move, the leaf arms dangle and reach out to kidnap me, to take me again to their torture planet where the evil beast is waiting for me. I scream and scream until the evil kahuna swallows me whole into his gaping mouth, leaving my flesh and blood dripping from his sharp teeth. I fall into the beast's dark, whirling belly and then the world dies.

And then I remember Butterfly again. He has sent a "Pink Angel" volunteer to my bedside. He motions to her as I am crying silently. She looks furtively around, picks me up into her lap, opens her dress, and puts her breast into my mouth. I fall asleep at my Amah's breast once more. Peace returns. Butterfly is a good friend to me.

I opened my eyes. From the floor, I saw the tall Englishman above me, reaching down and assisting me to my wobbly legs. The room was empty except for the two of us. Everyone had left over an hour ago. He took me to a nearby cafe, where another member sat alone. Hot coffee revived me. No one spoke or asked me any questions. I was grateful for the silence. It had been only one in a series of many other deep and powerful experiences that awaited me in the years to come, encountering this contact with the Divine life force.

Only when this series of childhood traumas revisited me in the latihan did the revelation come to me that I was undergoing the deepest therapy, the spiritual therapy of my human soul. Major problems or barriers were of my own making, preventing me from attaining the truth of myself. My spiritual conundrum was that I was and I was not the cause of my own condition. I didn't cause my deformity, but this fate was tied up with my spiritual condition. Nor could I on my own volition bestow grace upon myself to bring my soul out of the grave of Lazarus.

It was years after doing this latihan that gradually insights about my own life took on another meaning—why I was the way I was, why I did what I did, etc. It didn't come in one big revelation of truth zooming down from heaven. Only when I was ready to let go of my arrogance of self-understanding, and all my opinions, that I truly felt the primal emptiness, the void within, about which no explanations existed.

Then, when revelations came, meanings were not polluted and contaminated by my own opinions and egotism. This new spiritual psychology didn't come from my readings and traditional training in psychology. Freudian analysis, academic psychotherapy, or training in counseling can't even begin to compete with God the therapist.

The Early Days

By the second week I had shaved all the hair on my body, arriving at the group latihan entirely bald-headed. Living in our isolated cabin in Big Sur, we were always in the nude, so I did my latihans at home in the nude. One time in the San Francisco group latihan, I felt my movements were restricted by my clothes, so I simply took them all off and continued in the nude. I heard a wild loud laughter by one of the men, but I ignored it and continued my own dancing and singing latihan. Just before Bennett called "finish", I put on my clothes and left the room. I heard someone calling my name and turned.

Another new member came up to me shaking his head and laughing, "Chung, I have to thank you."

Puzzled, I asked, "For what?"

He finally stopped chuckling, and blurted out, "From the beginning I just haven't had any kind of movement, so tonight I thought to myself, why can't I have some kind of movement? Out of nowhere I heard a voice inside me say, "Open your eyes and look in front of you." I opened my eyes and three feet in front of me I see this short, bald-headed Chinaman dancing and singing loudly—buck naked. That vision totally blew me away and I busted out laughing and fell on my knees. I couldn't stop laughing. Suddenly in that moment of laughter my arm shot up in the air by itself. "Thank you, Chung, thank you." From that day on he never stopped moving in the latihan.

In the few weeks after my initiation, I had done over a dozen of these spiritual exercises alone, as though I was hungrily consuming batches of delicious donuts. I could not wait for the next few hours to do another one.

Barbara, my wife, joined soon after and did in fact find it to be beneficial. It was certainly the most far out thing we had discovered up to that point, and it seemed to integrate our entire search. Later, I realized that the make-up of the people in that room matched the strange vision I had on that sunny, drowsy afternoon only a couple of weeks before.

Henry Miller and Alan Watts

I went to visit my friend, Henry Miller, who lived up on Partington Ridge; his Big Sur home overlooked the Pacific below. I thought he might be interested in this latihan experience. There was a downpour such as is only seen in Big Sur, thunderously terrifying and keeping tourists away, but a welcome blessing for its residents. I knocked on Henry's door. A gorgeous woman in a black turtleneck sweater, leotards, and long raven hair opened the door.

"Yes? Are you lost?" she quizzed, a warm smile with a glass of wine in her hand.

"Tell Henry the Chinaman from Shanghai is here," I quipped in my drenched clothes.

"Oh?" she giggled. "Henry, the Chinaman from Shanghai is here."

"Ha, ha. Yes, by all means let Chung in and pour him a glass of wine, darling. He must be exhausted from such a long walk half way round the world. Ha, ha." I heard Henry's high pitch laughter in the background.

"Hello, hello, come, take off your wet jacket. Just in time for some wine, yes?" Henry was always very friendly and funny. He introduced us, "Darling, this is Chung, the interesting school teacher I told you about. This is Eve. Isn't she exquisite—and sexy, yes?" I had to pull my eyes away from Eve's hypnotic sensuality, which began to arouse that sleeping beast within me. Henry was a non-stop chatterer just like his wild free-flowing writings I loved and admired, a living American legend, a poet, and a noble man. You had to interrupt him between sentences to get a word in edgewise.

In my excitement to share this latihan contact, I quickly interrupted. "Henry, I had the most incredible experience last week and…". Before I could finish, he quickly turned in his chair, framed by a large glass window overlooking the crashing ocean waves below and pulled out a book from a stack of new publications.

"I just received this new release from one of my publishers who thought I might be interested, and instantly I knew you would enjoy it," Henry said, grinning as he handed me *Concerning Subud* by J. G. Bennett. This was none other than the Englishman who first opened me to the latihan! His new book was what I had wanted to tell Henry about! In that instant I felt that Henry Miller was also a medium, a messenger, to bring certain persons and ideas together. Like special carrier pigeons, these selected individuals were intermediaries whose life's task was to help interconnect people.

Henry believed in and did not question the latihan's validity, but felt it was not the time for him now to join any spiritual group. He preferred to wait before trying it himself.

There was another man slouched on the couch. Henry turned and said, "Chung, I'd like you to meet my old drinking buddy, Alan Watts. Alan, this is my dear neighbor (only thirty miles away) originally from China, Mr. Chung." Alan turned without getting up, a half glass of wine in his hand. He was already drunk and it was only late morning.

"Jo-sun-nee how-mah?" (Cantonese for "Good morning, how are you?") Alan spoke in crisp, clear Cantonese as he waved his glass of wine.

"Jo-sun. How-ah." ("Good morning, I'm well"), I shyly responded in my broken Cantonese. It always embarrassed me when people spoke Chinese to me and I had to apologize for my shameful ignorance of my mother tongue. Alan was fluent in Cantonese, Mandarin, and Shanghainese. He was also an eminent scholar of the history, politics and culture of China and Japan. Alan was the executive director of the East West Institute in San Francisco—a real Asian scholar and noted translator of Zen to the West. His inebriation, like Henry's, seemed to have no effect on his quick wit and impressive genius.

I quickly turned away from Alan because I detected his quizzical surprise at my not continuing to speak in Chinese, which he obviously enjoyed. Although tempted, I refrained from mentioning my great admiration for his Zen books and from acting like most fawning fans in the presence of celebrities. To this day, I regret not obtaining the autographs of these two great American artists and geniuses whom I so admired.

Henry was such a gentleman. He made everyone feel at home. He quickly came to the rescue of my blushing face. "Hey, Alan, please pour our friend another glass of wine! Come, come!" I felt like I was in Paris of the 30's, with all the great masters of art. I expected Hemingway, Gertrude Stein, Picasso and others to walk through the door any minute.

I learned that Henry and Alan had been friends for years. Alan was often an invited lecturer in Big Sur restaurants and homes of the rich and famous. Alan usually stayed with Henry whenever he came to give his lectures. Often Henry, Alan, and other residents frequented the local hot springs in the nude. Somehow, many beautiful women appeared out of nowhere whenever either of these men was present. I guess their charisma invisibly and magically drew the fawning, young damsels.

It was obvious both men had been drinking and talking all night long and had not slept. The house looked and smelled like the Parisian bachelor's quarters Henry had described in his books. His writing desk, coffee table, and floor were littered with empty wine bottles and scattered books, books, and more books, manually written scripts, and stacks of half-opened letters.

Henry raised each unopened letter to the light, peeking at it like a child against the window's ocean view. "Ah, I bet this letter has a check or money order!" He excitedly tore it open and sure enough he was correct—a green check fell out. Henry enjoyed reading most of his fan letters, except the perfumed or very thick ones. He was a charming and witty gossip, sharing international celebrities' secrets with relish. He was a wine connoisseur and lover of anything oriental, especially Asian women—young or old, he loved them all. He was the American Baudelaire. I had not known until I saw his watercolor paintings that Henry was quite an artist, as well as a greater writer.

"Now that is the correct way," Alan remarked, "for every great artist to be honored with cold cash in every fan mail! I am envious. To my great misfortune, my own admirers tend to hide their blatant materialistic generosity from me—can you believe that?"

"Well, Alan," Henry gave me an impish wink, "it wouldn't be very Zen-ish on their part, would it?" Alan gulped down the remains of his wine and Henry replenished it, smiling. His eyes were forever twinkling, dancing, and laughing.

Alan continued, "Unlike Henry, my mail is filled instead with terrible *koans* and riddles by old theosophical ladies in their fruit-basket hats. Now had I, like my esteemed and clever friend, filled my scholarly writings with offensive plebian obscenities that would have infuriated our noble Calvinist Supreme Court, my books might have been banned and I, ignobly condemned and exiled like Henry, would not be as drunk as I am today, living in my impoverished houseboat in Sausalito, but a true rich bastard, a living legend of American literature—a rich, drunk poet."

It pained and saddened me to witness Alan and Henry like this, both concealing their gothic agony, Alan behind his sardonic mask and Henry's hidden torment covered with cheerful, witty humor.

Henry Miller's years of rejection by his own country had left alcoholic scars on his noble face, crevices created by many drunken nights. It was the same with other American greats, Hemingway, Ezra Pound, and Robinson Jeffers, who were acknowledged, embraced and loved by foreigners as gifted contributors to the arts. Yet, the only thing that they ever wanted and secretly yearned for was a simple acceptance and recognition by their own people in their own native land; to be loved and accepted for who they really were—dedicated artists who knew how to quest for and express the truth.

Henry leaned over and put his arm around his dear drunk buddy, "Ah, love cannot be passionate when absent of life's tragic suffering. Is that not what the Olympian gods are made of, my dear friends? Come, let us give a toast!" Alan staggered to his feet, smiling sardonically, and embraced Henry with genuine warmth. I joined their toast.

I needed to hurry back to Carmel to see Bennett, the Englishman, though I was torn, leaving these two giant beings on the magnificent cliffs of Big Sur. "Henry, I came to invite you to join us in Carmel," I blurted out, "Also you, Alan. The book by that Englishman you gave me? He's here. John G. Bennett." Henry explained the latihan to Alan, but both kindly declined the invitation.

Alan surprised me by personally inviting me to attend his Zen lecture that same evening. Noticing my astonishment, he quickly assured me that he would be even more eloquent if he consumed a couple more bottles before his lecture. But, he promised, he would gladly recommend his friends to attend the latihan in San Francisco. Alan kept his promise and sent some of his fans to the San Francisco latihans. He even invited me to his Sausalito houseboat, should I happen to be up that way.

We all bear-hugged each other goodbye. I did not know then that it was the last time I was to see Henry and Alan alive.

My cousin, the famous Chinese-American actress, Lisa Wong, who was later selected to play the role of empress in the award-winning film "The Last Empress", was one of Henry Miller's dearest Asian companions. A few years after my visit with Henry, I happened to be visiting Lisa and her husband in their lovely Hollywood home, when she informed me of his death. I regretted not corresponding with Henry and Alan, but felt they both must have gone to a far, far better place than they had ever known before. Like the ancient giants and prophets of man's former golden eras, these great American artists and rebels have now joined their ranks on Big Sur's Mt. Olympus. Perhaps their spirits can still be heard laughing, toasting and singing loudly, "Live life spontaneously and with passion from beginning to end, forever believing you are the truth, always in battle against falsehood and all known injustices against man, the land, and its creatures!" Adios, amigos. I prayed I would one day join them on the other side. May God bless and protect them and all tormented artists forever.

Later, the Englishman informed me that he too, had personally told several noted celebrities about the latihan, such as Madam Ouspenski (wife of Ouspenski, the early student of Gurdjieff), Krishnamurti, and other legendary individuals still living at that time. Although Jung was interested and had set up a meeting to receive the contact, he passed on before the meeting took place. But other celebrities were opened; Aldous Huxley, Eva Bartok, and Steve Allen, who interviewed John Bennett about the latihan on a long-playing record.

Unlike Anything Else

I was initially subjected to the most intense, erratic, and painful physical training, draining every single ounce of energy I had. It was as if someone had designed a customized basic training for me to work out all the kinks, blocks, and impurities that had accumulated in my life. But the astounding thing was that after only half an hour or however long I did the spiritual exercise, I did not feel tired, but rather more energized than before it started! In spite of all the crying and thrashing about, I emerged as if nothing unusual or remarkable had occurred. I felt more relaxed, lighter and easier to live with, and my tension and stress gone. And there were no bad after-effects. The contact had no prerequisites, no dogmas, no rituals, no study classes or seminars, and no required readings.

For me, the best of all was that I was left alone and free to experience my own self, and not told what I should experience, what to expect, or what attitude or behavior I should adopt. No priest, no leader or obligation to listen to preaching, sermons, moral lectures, or another's concept of what is and what is not the world of spirit and its relationship to me. There was no imitation gold-plated altar, cross, or statue, no faded yellow old photos, pictures, or art, no lit candles, bells or gongs, robes or chemical tap water splashing on my face, no eating the flesh or drinking the blood of some long dead prophet, no buying a sacrificial chicken from the supermarket, no smoking cheap drugs or passing a dirty, mouth-diseased peace pipe, no pretentious, mumbo-jumbo Latin liturgies or pagan rites with ankle bells and gongs and drums from the imports store, no dancing in circles, and no holding each others hands.

There was no forced attendance to listen to some southern ex-insurance-salesman turned-evangelist in his new C & R suit, screaming his well-rehearsed, too-oft-repeated biblical translations. No leader, no preacher, rabbi, priest, imam, medicine man or witchdoctor, no magi, bald-headed and bearded guru, no psychic healer with a 1-800 phone number.

No specially required subscription books, literature, weekly-monthly newsletters, magazines, or junk mail to my private residence. No guilt pressured, obligatory contributions or tithes or low monthly payments for something special every month, like another new temple, college, or clinic for starving children in some barely existent country.

The real surprise for me was the incredible and unexpected confirmation that what I had called the living unknown entity within me was in fact, my soul being awakened by a higher power. I was beginning to have an extra sense, starting to have that true spiritual experience I had searched for all those years. It was now becoming manifest. I was actually experiencing a mysterious profundity as a consequence of the contact with the Divine force beyond what my mind could prove or deny. Only the power and will of God could have done this. I was enormously grateful.

Experiencing the Man

Flash—the *man* is arriving at SF International Airport tomorrow morning.

In 1958, no one really knew anything about the man who first received the latihan in Indonesia. There was no written literature or pamphlets of any kind about him. Earlier, I had fervently wished I had lived in the eras when the legendary giants and prophets had walked the earth. What, I had wondered really happened to the daily lives of their disciples and close followers when a new religion was born? I had tried to find the answer, unsuccessfully, in the obscure university stacks when I had been a student.

My wish came true.

The incredible impact the latihan made on my life must be in some measure similar to that of the earlier disciples and adherents of their masters. My entire life was being turned inside out and upside down—totally and irrevocably altered. I began undergoing many internal and external changes. I was never the same after that. Is this what happened to those early disciples—they instantly dropped their fishing nets, gave up their normal work, and perhaps some even left their wives and children to follow the prophets?

What would happen in the reality of today's technological America if a contemporary, ordinary man arrived who was commissioned by a higher authority to bring a special message to all of mankind. Have you ever wondered how *you* would behave if you were in the presence of a prophet or messenger?

It was John G. Bennett and his Gurdjieff associates who had first invited and financed this man and his entourage to come to Coombe Springs, England, from Indonesia. He was known to Subud members as Bapak (literally father), a commonly used respectful term for older

Indonesian men. Bapak opened hundreds of Bennett's students to the latihan who happened to be attending his Gurdjieff workshops.

After Bapak was with them in Coombe Springs for six months, he sent Bennett ahead to San Francisco to prepare for his American tour. I was in the initial San Francisco group whom Bennett and his wife Elizabeth initiated into the latihan contact. Under Bennett's guidance, we had been practicing the spiritual exercise for about three months before Bapak arrived in San Francisco. I can tell you, his arrival was too awesome to recount in any logically understandable form. I can simply say that when it comes to incredible moments in my life's scenarios, this was, without doubt, the ultimate and most awesome phenomenon—way beyond what I could ever have imagined.

Hearing that Bapak was making his first visit to America, I went straight to the San Francisco International Airport, doing 80 mph all the way. I saw a row of cars at the International Terminal entrance, so I parked behind a black limousine and rushed into the terminal. A man was sent with a special message for all mankind, and he landed right here in 20th century America at San Francisco International Airport in June of '58!

Yup—I was right there when Bapak stepped off the airplane onto the tarmac! I even surprised myself by boldly rushing and pushing my small frame through the large welcoming crowd at the gate. I gave the officials some crazy excuse that I was the official rep who was to escort this special VIP. Before they could reply, I was already through the security gates.

I immediately recognized the *man*.

There was an unmistakable singularity in his presence; he had the air of one who is a true emissary sent by the highest authority from another realm. He was a man with a special delivery package of *something* to mankind. In his presence I felt my entire body reacting, automatically bowing. He paused at the exit door of the jet, standing there in a dark suit, with an Amish-looking black hat, his eyes surveying this new continent and its people. I could feel his warm and compassionate blessing. My legs buckled, feet frozen to the ground. I held back tears of joyous gratitude. A powerful love that I had never before experienced imploded within me. It was as if I knew him, recognized him from another time or space. Everything blurred—a blinding, brilliant reality beyond all obscurity. I thought I was going to pass out from the dizziness in my cottonstuffed brain.

My heart stopped momentarily upon apprehending this miraculous vision. I was frozen to the spot and nothing could move me except by command from the very top. With my eyes fixated on Bapak, I saw nothing else. I could see his shiny black Oxford shoes clearly when I bowed. But I was bowing not to the man, but to the radiance of holiness I felt emanating from his presence.

It flashed on me then. It was this sense of awesome power and authority and the magnificent rapture of the love it engendered in everyone that must have been experienced in those legendary visions that shocked and haunted the early disciples and followers of the prophets and messengers of old. They were all suddenly awakened and blessed by the same thunder-striking and earth-shattering impact as when Moses descended like a giant from Mt. Sinai, holding God's Ten Commandments for mankind. Or perhaps they felt it the first time they saw Christ walking upon the turbulent sea, hushing the storm with his raised arm. Or perhaps they felt something like it when they were blinded by the radiant golden light around Muhammad, riding his enormous majestic camel towards them.

Yet, when seen from the perspective of ordinary reality, Bapak appeared outwardly so exceedingly common that he could've easily been invisible in any crowd. Whereas everyone has a certain distinct personality that makes them unique, this man stood out because there was a distinct absence of ego; there was no "*I am*", or "*Look-At-MEness*". He nodded and smiled, but was unaffected by the celebrity aura we put on him. He did not walk in any affected manner, with hands in folded prayer like the Dalai Lama, or waving blessings like the Pope. He walked and dressed like everyone else, yet he appeared to me as if he were floating two inches off the ground and walking in slow motion.

It became clear to me now why those in the past who were nearest to the prophets and messengers often did not pass down written records, such as a daily diary or log. Yet, how did the impact of being with the prophet affect their personal and family lives. What kind of changes did they undergo? For me, it was impossible to take precious time off just to record what Bapak spoke about, much less how I felt.

It is much easier to write about this experience after a lapse of time— now some fifty years later. However, at that time, each moment was so miraculously intense and alive in its immediacy, that it would have been as if trying to shoot treacherous rapids while writing down what was happening. The raft would have crashed into the boulders ahead.

I told my parents and sister about my experiences. They wanted real evidence. So I invited them to find out for themselves. After a few weeks both my mother and sister did receive the latihan contact and did believe in their experiences. On his deathbed my papa asked for the contact, so I passed it to him. He died peacefully, our hands clasped together for the first time.

I had never been a follower or believer of any cult, guru or movement, spiritual or otherwise. I had been a spiritual loner, living in Big Sur at the time. If you had told me that someday I wouldn't be able to resist and would go directly towards this brilliant light like a moth to its death, I would not have believed you.

For years afterward, I could not relate my experiences. Even writing about them was beyond me. I felt a secret lingering, schizoid disbelief in this man, while also feeling a personal embarrassment to admit openly that I followed him across the world—not once, but several times. I've criticized personality-cult followers and yet I myself quit several jobs, went into debt, and left my family, just to be near this man. I can now appreciate disciple Peter's devotion to Jesus and his three denials that he was not one of the followers of Jesus as the latter was being crucified.

I always promised myself I would not do this again, but the next time he stepped onto this continent, there I was again, right next to him. Once, I was so embarrassingly close I had to excuse myself from the limousine as he entered. I kept reminding myself that I was an objective, well-informed critical thinker who was in touch with all the new scientific ideas and processes. How could I have possibly fallen into this absurd herd thinking about some prophetic messenger with a new religion? Another ritual on top of all that already existed?

Bennett Tests with Bapak

A few days before the arrival of Bapak and his party, Bennett and I were having a Chinese meal after the San Francisco latihan, in the best Chinatown of America. I had completely forgotten the time. I had not had such a ball for years, it seemed. *Living in isolation is beginning to get to me,* I thought.

I had a bunch of *haoli* kids to teach in the morning, so I zipped my family out of San Francisco like a jackrabbit shot out of a cannon. The freeway was empty.

It was very late, when suddenly the old Ford wagon just stopped and died. I guided the station wagon onto the shoulder. A huge cloud of smoke blasted out of the engine when I lifted the hood. We had no money and no food. How was I going to be at school in the morning? Barbara and I got out and sat on the edge of the highway. It was a quiet and peaceful night with not a sound or sight around. There was absolutely nothing we could do except pray and wait until daylight.

As I sat by the roadside, I began to feel a stirring inside. Before I knew it, I was totally engulfed by a huge vibration, moving my feelings to be wide awake. This force made me stand up and look around, then moved my legs to the station wagon and to look within. The two little boys were asleep, curled on top of each other in our large down sleeping bag. Just as I returned to sit down, I could feel the latihan slowly ebb away. In less than a minute, we saw a huge tow truck with its yellow lights zipping along the opposite side of the freeway. We waved and the driver waved back. Surely, I thought he must be heading home after a long hard day. But to our delight, we saw the tow truck make an illegal U-turn and head towards us. He pulled up and asked if we needed any help.

I asked him if someone had called him. "No," he said. "I just happened to be passing by, saw you, and thought maybe you could use some help."

"Thank God," we said.

Over the weekend, a friend fixed our car. The following week we made our usual San Francisco trip to the Subud group. John Cook greeted us with a huge hug. With a big, smug smile, John said, "Bennett wants to see you guys pronto." He laughed, "He'll blow your socks off. Go on, off with you—and be sure to come back to share-and-tell!"

The tall, distinguished Bennett, talking in his eloquent British accent told me, "When I heard from your friends that you had not arrived back in Big Sur, I felt I should immediately call Bapak, since the urgency overrode the lateness of the hour."

My feelings picked up quickly, goose bumps popping up and crawling all over my body. I could barely contain my excitement. Bennett explained that fortunately, Bapak picked up the phone on the first ring. Bennett said, "Sir, please forgive me for calling you at this late hour, but…"

"Yah, Yah, it is alright. What is it, please?" Bapak asked.

Bennett told him, "We have a Chinese school teacher and his family who drive 300 miles round trip from Big Sur to attend the two group exercises here in San Francisco. Can you hear me?"

"Yah, yah, OK here, you may go on, please?"

"I got a telephone call from their friends saying that they had not returned to Big Sur. We don't know if he and his family are safe or not, driving this late."

"Yah." (pause) "Good time for you to practice testing, yes?" Bapak replied. "Please, Bennett, close your eyes now, and try to receive with latihan about Chinaman and family, and same time I help test with you on telephone. Yah, ready?"

Bennett told me he then closed his eyes and said to Bapak , "Yes, I'm ready, Sir."

"Relax. Yah. More deeply. Yah, yah, good. Now, you feel the latihan. How is the Chinaman and family at this time? Let Bennett receive now." Bapak was silent for a moment and then said, "Yah, yah… Please let go of worry… Go deeper still, yah, yah… No holding back. Let everything go… Let the power of God move your soul and your body."

"It was amazing," Bennett told me as he fully described the experience. "I opened my eyes, turned my head left and then right, I took a couple of steps and bent down as if looking for something and then I smiled. At that moment I knew you were safe," he told me smiling and remembering. "Then I told Bapak what I felt."

"Yah, yah, very good." Bapak said and then continued, "Now I test with you also and try to receive if Bennett's soul can feel my receiving—yah?"

"OK, Sir." Bennett closed his eyes again and stood relaxed ready to receive the latihan.

After a moment of silence, "Yah, yah." Bapak breathed. "Yes, you receive?" he asked.

"Not too clear... but I did feel myself smiling happily... like they will be alright."

"Yah," Bapak said, "very good. Help come very soon to Chinaman... See, big truck come help! Yah, yah. Your Chinaman is receiving at the same time we are testing. My airplane comes to America two days late, yah? OK? Good night, God protect you."

Later, I related Bennett's description of his first testing with my having felt that vibration in which I stood up, looked around, and leaned over to look into the car to see my two sleeping sons. Bennett was able to receive that I was OK—Bapak actually saw the tow truck coming!

Bapak's First Latihan in America

It is unbelievable how many of us men cried unabashedly while with Bapak in so many different situations and places. It had never before happened to me, nor to many of the others.

During Bapak's first night of doing the latihan with the men, I was swept away by a beautiful crisis. In the middle of devotion, it was as if a huge whirling volcano exploded, filling the entire room. The roof was blown off. I looked up at the blue sky and saw a golden orange windstorm zooming straight at me. There was a flash, then some mighty force swept into my heart, and a gigantic wind lifted the whole room upward like a giant UFO. Towards the end of the latihan, I could hear gentle voices above my prone body. Bennett's voice said, "This is the same Chinese man from Big Sur who drives three hundred miles round trip to do latihan here."

"Yah, yah. Very deep, very strong heart." The man's deep, sonorous voice responded with broken English.

"Yes," Bennett agreed.

"Yah," the man continued, "He make good helper." (Bapak appointed helpers to help him care for the needs of new members.)

"Yes," Bennett agreed.

"Yah. Finish now," Bapak said.

I opened my eyes and raised my head. Bennett and Bapak were standing beside me. As if coming out of some long-forgotten dream-torment, I found both my hands holding Bapak's black shoe, wet with my tears. I got up and noticed everyone sitting quietly around the brightly lit ballroom. I had been the only person lying in the middle of the large dance floor. To my surprise, I felt no embarrassment and no one was laughing at me on that miraculous day in San Francisco, in the early summer of '58.

My Second Heart

During that summer, a sharp pain on the left side of my chest was becoming more and more acute. It had started about a week before and now a protrusion the size of a golf ball was causing me concern. I was about to see a physician when John Cook suggested I see Bapak. The next day I did as he suggested. As I sat down with Bapak, he asked that his daughter, Rochanawati, assist in diagnosing the protruding lump next to my heart.

Rochanawati came through the side door and sat before me. She placed one hand on the lump and the other on my back directly opposite. She told Bapak that the "second heart" of my human soul was developing quite rapidly, but that I should not be concerned, the pain would soon subside. I should not worry, but continue with my latihan, be patient, and not try to comprehend the unbelievable by using my intellectual curiosity.

In private, Dr. Zakir translated the full account of what Bapak had replied to Rochanawati. He said I would bring many to Subud.

To be on the safe side, I still thought it might be wise to see a doctor. However, I was pleasantly surprised when, a few days later, the swelling and pain disappeared as quickly as they had appeared.

In my first year as a university student, I had done weight lifting, gymnastics and hand balancing, so I knew what it was like for muscles to go through pain and stiffness as they grow and develop. It felt as though I was developing muscles inside my chest that were not outwardly visible. Then, I quickly forgot about it.

As my inner heart grew quietly, my outer life became more and more difficult and confusing. The many changes and experiences I was undergoing in latihan left me totally bewildered. I was confused because, although I was not doing anything injurious to others, I was experiencing terrible internal sufferings after spending time with others—which made no sense.

Never before had I been able to experience directly the state of the inner feelings of those around me. At first, I thought their sufferings were my own. Feeling depressed, upset, stressed-out, irritable, or uptight, I had not attributed these painful and uncomfortable sensations to their true owners around me. I could not separate what was mine and what was theirs. Later, I became aware that I was becoming a filter for other's states, and that it required constant diligence on my part to flush and clean this refuse out of myself before doing anything else. It was like washing one's hands after toxic exposure.

The same must also apply to working with the spiritually ill, but this idea had not previously occurred to me. How does one protect oneself from the psychological and spiritual burdens or problems of others? Old Sigmund Freud did not seem much aware of this problem. He taught that the therapist should remain absolutely neutral in the face of both positive and negative transference-feelings emanating from the patient. But was this not a rather heartless position? And look at the cure record of psychoanalysts today! Not good!

I don't recall ever reading in the Bible or Qur'ran how the early prophets and their disciples prevented spiritual contamination. Jesus may have been strong enough in spirit to love a prostitute, and the Prophet Muhammad even captured a jinn at one point, but what about us? How would we come out of such encounters?

As if I did not have enough painful problems of my own, I now had added burdens to contend with, for which I had no remedies. I felt impotent to help myself, much less others. If I could not even solve my own problems, what could I possibly do for others? This new social and spiritual responsibility haunted and disturbed me to no end.

There were a handful of people in the room when Bapak took the opportunity to remind us, especially Westerners, not to continue our habit of using our mind and its intelligence to analyze the meaning of what each of us had experienced in the early phases of our latihan contact. He said that full understanding would eventually be achieved by each of us in our maturity, each in his own time. So much for my problems! Let my human heart grow!

Aloha, Big Sur!

At the end of that summer, I knew that my time in Big Sur was at an end. I bid aloha to the *kahuna* of Big Sur. As I walked up the silent, hot hill behind our Big Sur cabin, I continued doing the latihan, singing loudly beneath the expansive umbrella of the pure blue sky. *Aieee, ah-Ieiiii, wah-laha mai kawana luu kamay hah-ee wai-lu ha-ow.*

Half-naked, my bald head and tanned body glistened with sweat as the cool mountain breeze swayed the giant redwood tree branches. Blue jays alerted others with their high-pitched squawking at the Chinaman's coming.

At that moment, I was the first man, humanity, without a name.

Need I define who and what I am? Do the bird, deer and fish question their own identities? Had I ever heard a fly buzzing, "Who am I and what is the reason and true meaning of my buzzing?" Is there a presence that demands or expects a confirmation of my existence other than myself? I see no clone of myself. I have no need for language, for there is no one here to communicate with. There is no use for books, bibles, or any media. Like the rest of the other living creatures, I am not envious nor do I have a need or reason to compare myself to those with wings soaring in the air, those swifter than I with four legs, fur and claws, nor those who breath beneath the seas and lakes.

Guiltless and without question, I am whatever and whoever I am or am not. I have no need or want of ideas, concepts, premises, theorems, axioms, or belief systems to lean-on, to defend or to stand-on. I need no illusory hand-me-down ontological myth to confirm, deny, or explain the existentiality of being or non-being. Without proof or evidence, I am nobody and everybody, one and the same as the many, the many the same as I—a solitary creature without a tail, without wings and without gills. I can growl, hum, whistle, mumble, squawk, imitate, and act like any of the creatures around, above, or below me. I cry, laugh, sing, eat, or sleep as I am moved, as I breath.

It was already night; the sun had long been engulfed and swallowed by the horizon's edge when I descended from the Santa Lucia Mountains. The latihan this day felt as though some of my genes had by serendipity made laser contact with a forgotten hard disk that revealed ancient and secret recordings of historical happenings, eons before the great flood had wiped-out the first human race. Could it be that man's feelings of events are, like matter, indestructible, and that these gene-feelings do continue to exist from one's ancestry down to the present, and are then passed down to one's descendents, ad infinitum?

If so, then likewise do the dark feelings, the sins of our ancestors, also live and descend through the generations? Is it true that the sins of the fathers shall be visited upon the sons unto seven generations? I did not wish to dwell on other spiritual possibilities, such as the genes of the planet earth, its forests, and all the living creatures and their ancestral fossil spirits. Suffice it that *all* things have a life within themselves.

I came down the mountain and bid aloha to Big Sur *kahuna*. So long, Big Sur. may other seekers of truth take refuge and solace in your bosom. I shall never forget you, dear friend. Aloha with love, *kahuna* Sur. I left my *mojo* on her cliffs.

Summer of '58 – San Francisco

It was the season of what I have considered, to this day, to be the first American spiritual renaissance—a socio-political spiritual revolution that would eventually spread and alter the landscape of American consciousness for the next century. It brought out the worst, the best, and the totally unexpected in all and everything.

Arriving in San Francisco after leaving Big Sur, I moved my family into a beautiful, spacious ground floor apartment in the Haight Ashbury neighborhood, only half a block and across the street from the notorious Bagel Shop. The Bagel Shop restaurant was San Francisco's waterhole, the fountainhead of what was to become the breeding house of the American spiritual renaissance—the 60's movement.

Everyday I would get up and spend the whole day in that coffee shop, my second home. There I met Eric Nord, the biggest man I ever knew, who was over seven feet tall and 650 pounds in body weight. Eric was the self-appointed bouncer of the Bagel Shop. It was a microcosm peopled by unkempt, long-haired bohemians, people of many colors and life styles, homosexuals, lesbians, the divorced, the lost and unwanted, seekers and addicts, and the lonely hearts of America. Existential poetry readings, exhibits of new artists, new writers, and singers all came to the Bagel Shop.

Out-of-state tourists began coming by the busload, the "look-at-em" middle classes from Kansas, Texas, Montana, and elsewhere in middle America. Gradually, American youth began dropping out of school, running away from home, and hanging out at places like the Bagel Shop. They came from all over the USA, and even from foreign countries, to join the new spiritual renaissance in San Francisco. Leaders of the changing consciousness, Alan Watts, Mort Sahl, Joan Baez, Bob Dylan, and dozens of others came to the Bagel Shop. Many visiting gurus and Eastern mystics, students and their university professors, artists, musicians, and intellectuals invaded the area. It was the new Paris, USA, Greenwich Village West. San Francisco exploded overnight.

America, home of the free, was never to be the same again. Her sons and daughters had decided to stop following the unquestioned conditionings of the 1950's and the material-security obsession of their parents.

Elvis was still alive, shaking-up the flag-waving, Protestant-ethic middle-class with his revolving pelvis, opening wide the eyes of awakening young rebels to his sexual rock 'n roll beat. The unknown Beatles were just then turning London upside down, and would soon be on their way to America for their first world tour. At Harvard University, Professors Timothy Leary and Richard Alpert (who later became Ram Das) were then experimenting with LSD.

Bing Crosby and blue-eyed Frank Sinatra faded from the popular radio stations and disappeared off the top 10 charts, only to be replaced by the rock 'n roll invasion that came, conquered, settled and flourished in the new sexual freedom movement that dramatically and irrevocably altered the American psyche.

American universities exploded with campus riots, sit-ins, and dropouts. The Free University started up in Stanford and spread to UC Berkeley and San Jose State. From a little coffee shop in San Francisco's North Beach, and such places as the Fillmore Auditorium where rock 'n roll's best came to perform, the spiritual renaissance of America grew and spread to the University of California at Berkeley, down the coast to Stanford University in Palo Alto, then on south to Los Angeles, and eastward to the Atlantic coast—Harvard, Yale, Tufts, and then to New York City. It ultimately impacted the entire nation, igniting the flames of civil disobedience, inspiring marches for equal rights for all people, and protesting that genocidal war in Vietnam that was wiping out an entire generation.

The puritan walls of American sin-guilt imprisonment and inhibition collapsed. Libido was set free from Pandora's box. Young women waved their bras like flags of victory, wildly dancing nude in public, nymphs in open, free sexual revolution. Cocktail-boozing Mr. and Mrs. Robinson swore the sky was falling down.

This period lit the candle of America's youth. It was the arising of the American bohemians, artists and intellectuals with long hair, sandals, and worn blue jeans, who were later to be named the beatniks of the '50s, then transformed into flower-children and hippies who consumed illegal substances and sang accompanied by guitar, bongo drums, and burnt incense. The 60's became a new American consciousness in the making.

Meanwhile, I helped spread the latihan in the Bagel Shop and brought many beatniks to the latihan room.

My own latihan began spinning my body round and round and round, like a Sufi whirling dervish. The room of people would spin into a blur. This felt relaxing and had a calming effect. I was aware that my thoughts ceased flashing past my mind. Then, at first quietly, then louder and louder, I heard my voice come alive with strange noises, as if learning to speak for the first time. It spoke in incomprehensible guttural gobbledeegook utterances, much like speaking in tongues. I heard and felt myself manifesting loud, outward expressions of anger, rage and confusion, even accusatory cursing in ugly sounds and growls, like some hairy Neanderthal or abominable Asian snowman.

My entire being and psyche became a sacred temple exhibiting a historical psychodrama, purifying the sins of my human ancestry. I've never suffered more intensely than going through this cleansing phase of my own Chinese culture as well as mankind's injustices to each other, to nature, to other small and large creatures, and worse, to myself. I'd studied the history of man and his civilizations, but now I was living out the experiences in my flesh, feelings, mind, and soul. I now had a tiny but real sense of the tormented meaning of the crucifixion of Christ—his sacrifice, his suffering to redeem the sins of all mankind, the unbearable suffering that pushed him to the edge of his own faith to cry out, "Father, why hast Thou forsaken me?" I believe that I then traversed beyond ordinary schizophrenia into a sort of divine madness.

Being an American transplanted from China to the Hawaiian Islands, my historical cleansing experiences were culturally more Asian. My grandfather was one of the early Chinese who had worked in the sugarcane fields of early Hawaii and he had escaped. After being caught, he was moved to forced labor on the transcontinental railroad, but again he managed to escape. He found gold near the Truckee River and then snuck the gold back into China.

Other haunting images loomed in the latihan exercises as if from another realm, invading my consciousness—wars and plagues, intolerable suffering from famine, long lines of fleeing war refugees, abandoned children crying for their mothers, fires of destruction with the poignant odor of gunpowder and burnt flesh. In the latihan, I found myself chanting and sweating, hoeing and planting rice, with visions of rows upon rows of coolies in the scorching sun.

Much later my mama told me some of the horrors and sufferings she had witnessed as a young girl in China in the late 1800's. Many of her remembrances matched the tormented scenarios I had experienced in my latihan visions. The horrifying truths ran goose bumps of fear up my spine. Often at the end of forty-five minutes, my exhausted body was drenched in cold sweat. Yet, after a few minutes, I would feel totally refreshed, light-hearted and filled with renewed energy. Not wanting to frighten or prejudice my wife, I didn't tell her many of the uncanny and terrifying experiences I had, because they were my own karmic burdens.

Before encountering the contact with the great life force, I had dedicated my whole life to the search for true self-enlightenment. But to my utter astonishment, after the latihan, I felt my life shift strangely into reverse. Instead of pursuing my destiny, my past life was drawing me towards it like a powerful magnetic force I had never known or experienced before. Since I wanted to test the validity of the latihan in my own way, I let go of my whole outer life without trying to stop this reverse action. In this way, I would know in twelve months if this latihan was true, or another "crock", like many of the other guru-cult movements.

Reading the Bible in Humboldt County

Unable to find employment other than public school teaching, I was forced to return to that. By then, it was already a month into the school year and I didn't think there would be any positions open. But no sooner had I given up the prospect than I was called. An emergency illness had left an opening in Northern California, in Humboldt County. It was a small three-teacher school in a lumber mill village, where I was to teach the 4th and 5th grades to a bunch of wild, rough children of the lumberjacks who were responsible for cutting down the beautiful, giant redwood trees of California. It was an isolated community much like the wild, wild west of the early California gold rush. Many of the parents were alcoholics—fathers and mothers alike. Every night, my student's parents drank at the local tavern. Drunken brawls, fistfights, and gunshots could be heard nightly. Feuds, clashes, abuses of all kinds, especially from cuckolded husbands, were common. It was the dirtiest, loudest, foulest town I had ever lived in.

No matter how often Barbara cleaned our home, in a matter of hours it would be totally covered by sawdust from the nearby sawmill. It was easy to understand why these wild Americans turned into hardhat, right-wing, wannabe cowboys, roaming and howling nightly in their mud-covered jeeps and pick-ups. In order to stifle their boredom and fill their inner emptiness, as well as to deafen the constantly screeching sawmill blades, they were forced to get stinking drunk to keep their sanity.

I tried to distract myself by continuing my former reading of spiritual books, but it didn't work. I had lost all interest in "The Quest". What had once excited me was now boring and tiresome. I gave a whole truckload of books to the local library and in turn, borrowed a much worn Bible.

The last time I had read fragments of the Bible was when I was fourteen years old, a choirboy in Saint Peter's Episcopal Church in Honolulu, Hawaii. I had joined the church choir because I wanted to carry the big cross on the long pole down the aisle. Secretly, I also wanted to be near

Norma Chang, a cute girl in the choir, whom I was crazy about. Norma ignored all my attentions and instead was attracted to my good-looking brother, Ben, two years my senior. But Ben was interested in another girl. Life marches on.

I read the Bible from cover to cover. Every night, I would practice the latihan contact and read the Bible. For several months on end, I found myself out like a light, flat on the floor. My latihan had changed and I was no longer making wild animal sounds, yelling and screaming, only singing and sleeping throughout the whole experience.

I began wondering if I had lost the contact since little seemed to be happening. But whenever I had doubts, somehow I felt I should be patient, continue to trust, and not try to figure out the reasons for what was happening. So I carried on, trying not to fall to the floor and sleep. But after a few minutes, my knees would automatically bend, my body would fall, and for the next hour or three I would be out. Then I would wake up and crawl into bed. This continued for weeks and months.

However, the "sleep latihan", as I called it, was unlike my regular nightly sleep. Even my dreams were different from my regular sleeping dreams. They were deeper, as if safely hidden and shielded from my probing mind. The latihan contact had moved like a submarine, diving deep down, even below my unconscious strata, beneath secret depths where another was being spiritually breast-fed and nurtured, beyond the detection of my mental radar and the geiger counter of my sensitive feelings.

At work, I no longer taught as I had in Big Sur's one-room schoolhouse. Instead, I taught the three "R's" and other civic subjects and assigned regular homework as the other teachers. Needless to say, I knew my teaching days were coming to an end. It was no longer my cup of tea and I could not wait for the school year to end.

I noted further interesting phenomena while reading the Bible and doing the latihan. I had not experienced anything like it before. I began to sense another reality hidden behind the parables and allegories which I couldn't put my finger on. It felt as if I were actually living in that era with Christ, experiencing what he and his disciples were going through. Something very deep and profound vibrated in my being, but I didn't have a name or category for it. I began reading other author's interpretations of the Bible, but I couldn't find any connection or resemblance to what I was picking up.

This baffled and excited me and I became aware that something important was being communicated to me. Unlike most books, the Bible seemed to be filled with living spirits. It was as though the Bible's meaning possessed a real power to reach out and touch something profound in the depths of my being.

I don't know why, but the disciple Judas held a special fascination and mystery for me. I sensed that Judas Iscariot was very special, that he symbolized something that was not commonly understood. The biblical stories became like Zen koans or puzzling mysteries of Sufi stories I'd read in my earlier days. Since Christ knew how and when his appointed hour would come, then he must have knowingly selected Judas to be one of his disciples. Judas must also have known the real meaning and purpose of his selection and been a very aware person whose destiny was interconnected with his master's.

Who was Judas? And why were there twelve and not ten or fifteen disciples? Why were all these truths hidden and concealed behind parables and strange allegories? There is always a special reason when truth is concealed. If these truths are so important for mankind, then why not be up-front, open, and clear, instead of so mysterious that no ordinary common person can understand?

The government and its CIA and FBI have concealed certain top secrets, such as information about UFOs, to "protect" the public "for its own good" i.e., to prevent national panic and chaos. Is the Bible doing the same? If so, why? Knowing that man is in a bad predicament and is desperate for the truth, why not be frank, direct, and open, if the truth really does bring peace of mind?

This led me to check out old fairy tales and fables. I began to re-read many of the Aesop's fables, Alice in Wonderland, and fairy tales from other cultures. I discovered that these children's fables also concealed truths behind mysterious allegories.

I came to realize that there is a reason and purpose why spiritual truths are concealed behind parables, riddles, miracles, and allegories. Only when one's soul has grown and matured will the mysteries of the spiritual conundrums be revealed. But, meanwhile, I had to be patient and simply accept without analyzing.

Before my exile in my private Siberia (Humboldt County) came to its end, I kept wondering—why was I exiled to this godforsaken place, reading the Bible without true spiritual understanding, and living among people who had desecrated the land to the foulest and dirtiest degree imaginable?

Without the Angel Gabriel, I had to visit and tour one of the dimensions of hell. I could not help but see the resemblance of this village to those of the many Biblical stories whose people had suffered terrible consequences from being dominated and governed by their passions, desires, and falsehoods. With all the freedoms, vast natural resources, and opportunities in today's America—all this and more did not make any difference to the crazy idiots in this town. People having much less are much more spiritually advanced than they. The residents of Humboldt are the direct descendents of the early settlers of the Wild West. Is the Bible a mirrored reflection of what's happening today, and not simply fictional stories of some forgotten era of mankind?

At first, I had felt guilty and helpless for not doing something to help change the lives of these people. But at the same time, I knew I was not ready to combat, single-handedly, the widespread human corruption surrounding me. I could barely defend and protect my own self and family from this insidious plague.

At this period in my life, I needed to witness for myself what happens to people when their lives are governed by their passions for alcohol, anger, and violence, have no regard for morality, no serious and genuine interest in self-enlightenment and spiritual growth, no respect for preserving and appreciating wildlife and nature, have no compunction about abusing women and children, and who have absolutely no reverence for life.

Most weekends Barbara and I would take our two boys on a drive. We spent a lot of time in and around Arcata, the Santa Cruz of the north. By now, it had become our practice to keep the latihan alive and on the front burner everywhere we drove, stopped, and visited. We both loved Arcata and felt it was a good place to live, so we checked out several rentals. But it was too long a drive for me to go to work every day. We could only hope to move to Arcata later— which we did several years afterwards.

Soul's Chosen Destiny Revealed

A rumor reached us that Bapak was on his way to make another appearance in San Francisco in the upcoming summer. No sooner had I received my last paycheck than I leaped into our car with my family (which my wife had already packed the week before), and drove at mach 2 speed straight out of town.

Before the sun touched the horizon, we were happily consuming our salty fish and chips on Fisherman's Wharf in San Francisco, having escaped our Siberian exile. We savored the blazing sunset and the cool, fragrant salt air on our smiling faces. Our two boys, Tama and Caleb (now three and four years old), threw bread crumbs in the air and laughed with delight as the seagulls squawked, snapping the crumbs in mid-air dives. Their mother and I joined their screeching and giggling as San Francisco winked her city lights, blowing her fog-horn-nose loudly for all to hear, while these four Siberian refugees gave great belches of gratitude.

Just for the hell of it, I decided to treat my family to a crazy luxury. I drove our dirty, luggage filled car up to the uniformed doorman at the St. Francis Hotel atop the famous Snob Hill. In my worn jeans and old cowboy hat, I walked up to the gilt-edged mahogany counter and handed green cash for two nights stay to the shocked, falsely-smiling desk clerk. We were whisked up in the gold leaf mirrored elevator to our suite with a separate living room over-looking the Bay and Alcatraz Island. We all yelled, "Yahoo, here we're, folks! Like it or not, the Chungs are on top of the hill!" We felt like the Beverly Hillbillies.

The two boys quickly opened the window and began making and flying paper airplanes down to the tourists on California Street. Barbara dropped her dirty traveling dress on the white-tiled floor and jumped into her first hot bubble bath in twelve months, in a real bathtub with gold faucets. I instantly reunited with my naked kanaka beach-comber (except for my cowboy hat) and sat in the elegant royal blue chair with bare feet on the marbled windowsill. I read my first San Francisco Chronicle in a year, overlooking Chinatown's sultry lights and the great bridge.

A knock on the door and in came a white-clad waiter behind our family dinner with two dry martinis with olives on a toothpick. *Ah, it's all hanging out now*, I thought, *my ancestral imperial Chinese arrogance.* Although it was the beginning of summer, I had the room clerk light the fireplace we had in our living room. He did, smiling knowingly, pleased also with the generous tip my son, Tama, gave him. I didn't know the kid was going to give him a twenty-dollar bill! Oh, well what's money for! Meanwhile, Caleb seemed much too quiet in the bedroom. We soon discovered he was throwing seven dollar French fries to the pigeons!

It is interesting that after I began the latihan contact, those formerly well-disciplined little boys appeared to become wilder and wilder. Naturally, I didn't tell them that their mom and dad, in their twenties and thirties, were just as wild if not more so!

The following week, Bapak landed in San Francisco on his second world tour and stayed for a month before going to Los Angeles. My good friend John Cook was also present again. I always enjoyed John's many gossipy secrets from the "inner circle" that always surrounded and followed Bapak. He spun his wheelchair around and whispered, "Psst, Chung, wanna hear something?" With our bald heads close together, we must have looked like the eight and cue balls for someone to sink easily in the corner pocket.

"You know I'm always a sucker for hot juicy gossip, man," I smiled. "Will it make us even?"

"Stick around for the late-night show again, man, " John chuckled conspiratorially. During the previous year's visit, a small group of us had been privy to the man's talks until dawn. For some reason Bapak usually did not sleep at night and would come down stairs. If anyone was present, he would spontaneously tell some stories and adventures of his spiritual life and other interesting and astounding secrets of the great prophets of ancient times.

Bapak always gave long nightly talks to the large group, but the late night talks going on until dawn—only a few of us were lucky enough to attend in the early days. This, John believed, was an extra goody for those who did the sleep-fast, a practice that I was accustomed to.

One evening, John Cook and I went to have noodles together in Chinatown. We chatted and laughed until one in the morning and then drove back to where Bapak was staying. John told me to be near the door that Bapak would eventually come through. At the right moment, if I dared, he said I should ask him for my true spiritual name and my true work.

"What?" I was taken aback. "But I have a name already, though no one ever pronounces it correctly."

John asked, "What does your Chinese name mean, Chung?" Always slightly embarrassed when asked this question, I quickly blurted out, "Chung Tien-Yau means the 'Bells of Heaven. "

"Hmm very exotic name, but too hard to remember for us *haolis.*" He continued, "What are your plans since you're not going back to teaching?"

"I'm thinking of going back to graduate school to do doctorate studies in psychology," I shuffled hesitantly.

"You don't sound certain," John replied looking directly into my eyes. "Chung, listen," John continued, "the old man has been giving spiritual names for those who wish to have one and it really makes a difference. He has only done this in his own country, not in America as yet. But I'll bet once the word is out, there will be a mad rush in America for new names. Besides, what've you got to loose? You don't have to use the new name, and knowing your independent nature, you probably won't even follow his suggestion of what you should be doing anyhow. So…?"

"And what's the new name he gave you?" I snapped back.

"I'd rather not say," John mumbled sheepishly, turning away.

"Oh, really now?" I paused. "OK, but I can't promise I will do it," I tried to set up a face-saver for back up. As a kid, I was constantly picked by the other kids for every cockamamie dare. Fool that I was, I could never seem to resist. The exhilarating rush was too enticingly scary for me to turn down. The unexpected surprise was worth taking the risk of the unknown. I rationalized to myself that if my appointed hour was not imminent, then I must be immortal until that inevitable moment, which I couldn't control anyhow. Perhaps I was a masochist, or crazy, or both. I noted John's eyes twinkling as he observed me intently.

"I know you'll do it," John confidently predicted.

"I didn't say yes—but I might consider it." That familiar *deja vu* trembling returned from my childhood, the ecstasy of terror, that most sensuous temptress. I was helplessly aroused by her mystic, sultry powers.

We waited and waited with the others. Just when part of me started wishing the man was asleep and not coming this time, he appeared in the doorway that I was leaning against. I felt his enormous presence and turned. There he was, big as life, only two feet from me!

I nearly jumped out of my pants, turning into John's wheelchair. I felt him elbowing me. I ignored his signal.

I took a deep breath, nearly choking on my half burned cigarette, my legs shaking as if I were about to make a Kierkegaardian leap of faith. I wiped my moist hand on my head to brush back my long black hair, forgetting that I was balder than the extinct Chinese eagle! Before the words came forth from my dry mouth, the stranger turned and looked directly at me and smiled, "Yah?"

I went into shock, totally surprised because I was certain I hadn't said anything yet. His interpreter looked at me as if to say, "Well?"

Quickly, I blurted out, "Excuse me, would you be so kind as to tell me if I need to change my name?" I thought I had cleverly asked two questions by throwing only one stone, thinking he would be induced to not only to tell me my new name, but its meaning if I needed it. If he should reprimand me, I thought, I'll accept the consequences.

"Yah, yah." The old man closed his eyes and raised his head upward, then replied, "Yah, your soul is, ah..." he turned to the translator and spoke in his strange, melodic tongue. "Ah, yah, yah, soul like a desert—new name bring needy rain to grow. Yah, hmm …yah, you Sam-Tio."

The translator repeated, "Sam-Tio is the name of your true soul. When others call your new name, it's sound will attract and bring you what your soul needs now. OK, Sam-Tio?"

"Thank you," I answered, and quickly stammered, "Then is it alright for me to return to the university to pursue my doctorate in psychology at this time?" Again, another quick two-questions-in-one.

Bapak gave out a hearty laugh, and turned again, talking with his interpreter. I choked and thought to myself, *uh-oh, I'm gonna get it now for sure.* I heard something about "Chinese", "broken car" and "doctor".

I asked the translator, "What did he say?"

"He was just confirming if you were that same Chinese man whose car broke down the last time we were here." The translator confirmed to him that I was that same person.

"Yah? Yah. Hmm...uh, guru. Yah, Sam-Tio is guru," the man smiled pleased.

Now I was really confused. I knew guru meant "teacher", but I didn't like teaching kids. I had planned to drive back to my former university in the Midwest for my doctorate in psychology. I asked the translator if Bapak might be, perhaps, a bit off?

He looked serious and stern as he and his translator spoke in their own tongue. I felt I must've blown it. The interpreter calmly said; "He did not mean schoolteacher with children, but guru—spiritual teacher, do you understand? Yes, you may go back to the university, but you must drive more carefully this time, yes?"

"Ha, ha, yah, drive slow," then turning to his interpreter he spoke to him again. The interpreter turned and said to me, "He said to inform you that you can later return to California because your true work will be wherever you are."

I was not only stunned, but totally bewildered. I personally had an aversion for foreign gurus, their cult followers dressed in colored robes, repeating robot-like mantras, performing their rituals with bells and drums. I had been looking for a guru in my early twenties, now I wondered had the guru been within me all this time?

At the end of that summer in San Francisco, I drove my family very slowly to Missouri. This time I did drive safely and arrived in Columbia without any mishaps.

The Power of a Name

I had no idea who this Sam-Tio Chung was. Like a mother rocking her new-born baby, wondering what her precious child would be like when he became a grown adult, I had no idea what destiny lay in the future for the new Sam-Tio, my identical spiritual twin brother. There was nothing I could do except stand aside and simply observe, and let go of everything.

But wasn't there an inevitable tragedy when this earnest, young seeker of truth became the betraying Judas who gave the sleeping Tien-Yau the kiss of death, so that his soul, named Sam-Tio, would arise and live?

Tien-Yau had up until then, never known, read, or heard that souls actually manifested in reality, grew, developed, went through phases, and eventually matured into adult human souls. People, as far as he knew, either did or didn't have souls. And one was either saved or not saved—period. He had never found any writings in philosophy, psychology, mysticism, occult, or any biography or autobiography of any spiritual leader that had ever hinted at or described the growth and development of a human soul, much less its transformation into a higher soul. Obviously a soul doesn't just pop up as an adult soul out of nowhere. Is it possible that baby souls are born, crawl away and hide, are secretly nurtured, protected, concealed and watched over by God, while they grow to adulthood?

It came suddenly but quietly, this missing secret piece of the puzzle—a piece that fitted perfectly. *By every shadow's edge, by the presence of its absence is the truth revealed!* This made logical sense of all the religions, mystical conundrums, parables, and myths, and why we cannot fathom the meaning and purpose of why we are here.

God in His wisdom not only created souls, but made them eternal and distinctly separate from the physical bodies of their hosts. Souls come in many different shapes and forms, from material souls to human and higher-than-human souls. As all biological life-forms require food and nourishment to grow, develop, and mature, so also do souls progress, grow, develop, and transform into higher souls, but only via a *process* that truly deepens the soul's worship of God. To worship is the process by which the soul grows.

Tien-Yau had promised himself he would give the latihan contact at least a year to prove its spiritual value or he would drop it and continue his search. It had been less than a year since he left Big Sur. He had kept his word. Sam-Tio was in a cocoon from Oct '58 to June '59. The Humboldt experience gave him a job and kept his mind busy reading the Bible, rather than thinking about the latihan. Something was germinating. He learned patience; like a child's development, his own soul's development couldn't be pushed.

The Unscheduled Opening
of Leonard Meyers

Here's how my friend Leonard Myers came to be opened. Before meeting Bapak in San Francisco, I had remembered Leonard Meyers, whom I had met in my university days. We had shared a common interest in spiritual and psychological ideas and had had many all night discussions. I had promised to write and inform him whenever I happened to come across some new ideas and so I did.

I had purchased one of the new long-playing tape recorders, a Wollensack. I began recording a tape letter one night telling him about my self-study with Gurdjieff, Zen and Sufi books, my 21-day food fast (except water), going without sleep and sex, and long hours of meditation. Finally, I began doing the actual latihan on the tape, particularly the singing part, which lasted over an hour. I wrapped the tape reel and mailed the package to St. Louis, Missouri.

Several months later, I received an urgent letter from Leonard's wife. She wrote that before my package arrived, her husband was intensely involved in oil painting and his guitar. But after my packaged arrived, he had simply stared at it on the coffee table. He had refused to open it for three days, which increased his wife's discomfort and anticipation.

Leonard was very stubborn and proudly independent, a fanatical individual of German ancestry. He resented being shown, taught, or told anything. His high standard was that he must discover and experience everything for himself before he could believe it. We had this attitude in common. At any rate, Leonard felt he must get the idea on his own before he would open my package, since he knew I would only communicate if I had something urgent to say.

Finally, his wife continued, Leonard decided to open the package and play my tape-letter. His wife said that afterwards, everything came to an abrupt halt. All he was interested in doing day and night was replaying the tape over and over again. He stopped painting, stopped playing the guitar, refused to eat, and no longer paid any attention to her, his children, or his friends. It was as if he died from the moment he opened the package. He did not leave the couch or clean up after himself. His hair and beard grew longer and longer until his head and face were covered with long hair, like Rip Van Wrinkle. He kept moaning, groaning, muttering nonsense, and making weird noises all day and night. Leonard's wife was deeply worried and asked if there was any way that I could help her husband. She felt something terrible and mysterious was happening to him.

A couple who had helped establish the San Francisco group and who were experienced in the latihan, were making a tour to Chicago at that time. I asked if it would be inconvenient for them to make a stop in St. Louis to see Myers. I told them about my tape and my belief that Leonard Myers had gotten the latihan experience directly from it, but did not know how to stop the action!

No sooner did the husband walk into Leonard Myer's St. Louis house than Leonard went into a wild, screaming, and jumping latihan. With no introduction, and without further ado, the man dropped his overnight bag at the door and joined Leonard in a spontaneous latihan.

Meanwhile, I was on my way back to Missouri. I enrolled in the graduate school at the University of Missouri, my old Alma Mater, where as Tien-Yau, I had earlier earned my B.A. and M.A. in philosophy and educational psychology. Just to play it safe and give it my best shot, I enrolled as Sam-Tio Chung, the new name that Bapak had given me. I must confess I checked the weather report now and then, hoping it would rain and fertilize some money-trees, as well as my newborn soul.

I could not help but wonder as to the real spiritual meaning of why I was, for the umpteenth time, returning to this same town, Columbia, Missouri. I felt as if I was traveling backwards in time, to where my spiritual search had begun five years before. We barely had enough money to secure a rental house across the street from the emergency entrance of the community hospital. Even with all my qualifications, I was turned down for all public school teaching. *Here we go again,* I thought. *Were the Missourians afraid their little kids would get yellow fever if they hired me?* So be it. I would have to come up with something else.

Immediately after returning to Missouri, I called my old buddy, Leonard Meyers. He and his wife arrived in Columbia the following week. The moment Leonard entered our new home with only the briefest of greeting, I noted that my friend was in deep crisis. I had never known Leonard to look so terrible, with an unkempt long beard and dirty long blond hair. The Leonard I had known was a plain dresser, nothing fancy, but always meticulous. He had the delicate hand of a lithograph artist. He was shy and spoke with a quiet voice. But appearance was deceiving with Leonard. He was a solid, slim, well-developed gymnast and handstander, strong in both physique and character. He was a folk song buff; he had sung ballads with his guitar and banjo for many hours while I listened, enraptured, as a freshmen at the university. Barbara directly ushered his wife to the kitchen in the back of the house.

Without any preliminaries or verbal exchange, Leonard closed his eyes and sat quietly on our old couch. It was a hot Midwestern night, around 11 pm, with windows and the door wide open. A large floor fan was whirling noisily next to the brick fireplace. I was sitting in a chair. In less than a minute, I felt a pain in my chest, constricted and tight, causing me to take short, quick breaths. There was also an unfamiliar trembling, as if I were walking on a swaying, taut high wire between two buildings, balancing a long pole.

My body sways as the fan blows a high wind. I am desperately trying to hold my breath and keep from falling to the ground below. There is no safety net. The silence is intense, and the spectators below are holding their breaths, their hands to their gaping mouths.

Almost imperceptibly, I feel the bottoms of my feet vibrating, like a mild California earthquake. I feel the monstrous beast has been rudely awakened in his deep lair in the center of the earth.

Leonard had stripped except for his briefs, his long slim taut muscles quivering in that hot summer night. His body leapt from the couch to the center of the living room, he was shouting and jumping up and down.

The pain in my chest zooms upward and my head feels as if it is about to explode. From the chair, I watch my body curl and fall to the floor. The spectators scream as the highwire gymnast falls off the wire, the long pole floating down alongside his body. The crowd instinctively backs into a widening circle as if making room for an unexpected guest. In slow motion, his body hits the ground with a thud, bounces, shakes, and is still.

My head was banging on the hardwood floor, and hearing a whirling fan overhead, I turned. The fan without wings flew against the wall and fell still whirling like an injured wingless bird. Leonard had picked up the floor fan and thrown it.

The long pole bounces out of the circle of the spectators.

A deep growling beast within me emerges and roars as it had done on Big Sur mountain. It has been asleep for over a year in the giant redwood forests. There is a deep base voice, slow and haunting, then changing into a long, wailing, sad song like a solitary primitive man who has lost his mate. The full moon lights the dark living room. Drum sounds and stomping bare feet like an Indian dance beseeches desperate rains to fall on the parched dry dust of our souls. Boom! Boom! Boom! Aiiee, aiiee, eii, iaee wal lahaaa....

On and on through the silent night. Missouri had never known or heard such strange goings-on since the many American Indians were massacred on its beautiful rolling hills and forests and flowing Mississippi Delta.

A loud knocking sound came from my front door. I thought it was my head banging on the floor. After about the third knock, because the doorbell was inoperable, I peeked through the front window curtains. Leonard was still yelling and jumping. I looked out the window.

Oh, my gawd! It's the police! And the whole neighborhood is out on my front lawn in their pajamas!

"Cool it! Stop! The cops are here!" I whispered. Leonard continued his latihan. I couldn't tell if he hadn't heard me or couldn't bring himself to finish.

I opened the door a crack. "Yes, officer?" I asked politely with a big innocent grin. I had forgotten I was wearing only my briefs, and that my head was bald as a cue ball. Being Asian gave me three strikes already, in addition to disturbing the peace.

"Open this door," the young officer snapped, his superior and another rookie behind him. The crowd stretched their necks, gawking.

The hell I will, was the thought I had. Still smiling, "What seems to be the problem? Do you have a warrant, sir?" I inquired.

My other hand waved at Leonard to stop, while trying at the same time to put on my cloths before they broke through the door. I had only just arrived in Dixieland and our luggage wasn't even unpacked! The old Hawaiian children's jingle rang in my head, "Oh fly, please don't ka-ka on me ... oh, fly please don 't ka-ka on me ... I promise, I promise not to do it again, oh fly, please don't ka-ka on me... 'cause you'll make me feel like a pile, like a pile of stinking ka-ka, oh fly, please don't ka-ka on me..".

"Listen," the belligerent young officer's loud voice was interrupted by the older officer who stepped forward.

"Excuse me," the Superior interjected quietly, "we would appreciate it if you would let us just talk to you, sir. We're responding to some loud noises that have been disturbing your neighbors. They were concerned that maybe somebody was being hurt or ....".

"Oh, alright. You can leave your shoes on, but take off your hats please. I'll be right back." I had to stall them while Leonard returned to sitting on the couch, but still without bothering to put on his pants.

I put on my pants but couldn't find a shirt. I opened the door to let the officers in. The young angry one stared at me like any pissed-off smart aleck who couldn't get his way. I returned his stare thinking *up yours too, with hot peppers, buddy.*

I graciously offered them the chairs that were upside down as if a hurricane had hit. I called to Barbara to bring some hot tea for these gentlemen. They politely took off their hats, except the smart aleck, until his Superior gave him an eye signal and he reluctantly obeyed.

Three hatless cops were now sitting and having a cup of late night tea, chatting quietly as if in London or China. One bearded, almost naked man was sitting on the couch, still rocking and swaying back and forth and a bald-headed Chinaman still had only his pants on. A floor fan lay on its side against a brick fireplace, still whirling the wrong direction; magazines, newspapers, books, dirty trousers and shoes, along with a broken guitar and a large bongo drum, lay scattered on the floor. It was two in the morning, and the pajama-clad crowd was still peering through the half opened door.

Strange sight? It didn't really occur to me then, but I was in middle America's Dixeland where not too long ago, blacks were hung just for spitting in their own hands.

I explained quietly that we were only doing a healing worship. I was tempted to say "to cleanse the state of Missouri of its abominable history of human injustice." We apologized for having disturbed our neighbor's much needed sleep, and we promised not to continue for the rest of the night. After double-checking the rest of the house for any peculiar goings-on, they departed satisfied with our tea and cooperative hospitality. An article appeared the following morning on the Columbian Tribune's front page, something like:

A Strange New Guru

Late last night the police were alerted to a mysterious commotion across from the Community Hospital that brought many neighbors out in their pajamas. Upon entering the premises, the authorities learned that the strange noises had been caused by a newly-arrived Eastern Guru and his follower's singing, chanting, and stomping, accompanied by drums, flutes, and strings of their new spiritual ritual. They were scantily clad but polite, and even offered oriental herbal tea to the admitted officers. Having been reassured that the new group would continue to assert their right to freedom of worship without further disturbing their neighbors, the officers departed. Since there was no crime committed, no arrests were made.

This story must have been retold many times, until the day we left Columbia three years later to return to California. Leonard Meyers returned to St. Louis, Missouri, about 150 miles east, in much better condition than when he arrived. He later moved with his family to San Francisco where he worked successfully and happily as a commercial artist. Leonard's wife subsequently asked to receive the latihan contact and they both continued doing the latihan with the Subud group in San Francisco.

I See the Face of My Soul

Before one memorable dawn in Columbia, I was awakened and felt a strong urge to do a latihan. Something fascinating clicked deep inside of me, a sound-wave flashed into my consciousness. Except for my sight, my entire body remained immobile for the next 30 to 40 minutes. Laying on my back in my shorts, I was transfixed as I witnessed the most astounding phenomenon.

A head popped up from mine, eyes staring at me. I saw the face of my soul, smiling at me in recognition. Slowly, he moved up as his chest emerged from mine, then followed with his legs coming out from mine. For a moment, he stood up, his feet in mine.

He walked to the center of the room, standing totally without clothes. He looked about my age, twenty nine, calmer, much more handsome, and taller, with his head also shaved bald like mine.

He began doing the latihan as I watched in awe. I felt the same movements in my body as he solemnly and gracefully danced, exactly as I would have. I wanted to get up and join him, but my body was frozen.

His voice began singing the same melodic tune I had recently been singing. For a brief moment my eyes closed involuntarily, but my body recognized and anticipated every movement a few seconds before he did his. It felt as if I was actually doing the same latihan exercise as he was.

The blood sped wildly through my brain, my heart racing as if I had been hit by a powerful thunderbolt. Suddenly, I knew love for my spiritual identical-twin brother, for whom I had been searching all these years. He knelt down in prayer form, then stood up and walked in front of me. I was incredulous when I noticed that he was not crippled. He stood erect and both legs were even. He walked normally, without a limp. Standing in my feet he spoke in silence to me, and I was surprised that my feelings clearly understood everything he was communicating.

He acknowledged that he was my human soul, conceived and created by the One Almighty God. He was pleased to join my destiny and be my loyal guide in life from that moment on. If I needed help, I had only to ask and it would be given. If I had any question or felt confused as to what course of action to follow, he assured me he would be here to help. He smiled, nodded, and reentered my body. My body came alive and I dressed. When I related this experience to my wife, she cried in happiness.

Inn of the "DUBioUS (S)elf"

While picking up the paper one morning, I walked into a corner cafe on Broadway, Columbia's main boulevard. It seemed as if I landed in two separate Americas. All parts north of Broadway were white. Separated by the railroad track that was like an invisible wall of hate, the south of Broadway was the ex-slave's world, the Negro's hell-hole, the "nigger town", confining and reminding them at every moment that they were sub-humans without human souls. There were two of everything, from restrooms to drinking fountains to bus seating (Negroes to the rear). Negroes couldn't eat at "for whites only" restaurants, but the outcaste could shop anywhere if he had hard cold cash.

Interesting in a shocking way, the sidewalks and paved roads literally ended on the white side of the railroad track. Dirt roads, dirt walking paths, potholes, mud and trash were everywhere on the other side, where the outcastes lived. But at least you could always hire a cheap house servant from over there—some poor Negro woman with kids from absent fathers.

I was the only customer in the deserted restaurant. Trying to be friendly, I remarked jokingly, "With this much business you should be out fishing on such a day."

The white, middle-aged proprietor answered without looking up, "Sure like to if somebody cared to buy me out, I'll be right on my way to the closest creek with my bait and tackle."

"Is that a fact?" I heard my own voice blurt out, more surprised than the restaurant owner. For a second I wondered what made me say that?

He sauntered up, wiping his large hands on his dirty apron. He reached in his pocket and slammed a set of keys on the counter next to my half empty coffee cup.

"Them there is the keys to this place. For $3,000 you or anyone else can have it now," he said without a blink. He was not joking. He was serious.

Again, I was shocked to hear the words tumbling out of my big, loud mouth, "Fair 'nough, partner, on one small condition if you'll agree."

"Depends—let's hear it" he twanged. "It's your wooden nickel, fella. Just you spit it out, I'm all ears, boy."

I rubbed my bald head as if I really knew what I had in mind. It was a blank. But before I could gather my thoughts, I distinctly heard my voice reply again. "You wait here, I'll be right back."

"I ain't plannin' to go nowhere," he answered with his back toward me. I went next door to a loan shark's office.

"Yes, can I help you, sir?" the suited manager asked.

"Yeah. I'd like to take out a loan for $3,000," I said, "Can it be done today?"

"I don't see why not," he smiled greedily, "with the proper papers. Do you have any references and what do you need this money for?"

"I plan to open a Chinese restaurant next door," I blurted, "I just came into town and I don't know anyone."

"Well, I'm sorry, sir, but the main office requires some kind of references," he said apologetically.

"I'll be right back," I said as I left.

What the hell am I doing, I thought to myself. *Making a pot of rice is the extent of my repertoire in Chinese cuisine.*

But then a brilliant idea struck me as I strolled down the street on that sunny day, the chilly Missouri autumn beautiful with its many colored leaves, like butterflies perched on their branches. Up the City Hall stairs I climbed with my limp. I walked to the secretary's desk and asked to see the city District Attorney.

"Do you have an appointment, sir?" she asked without even looking up, pretending to be busy with her papers. I knew she had seen me walk in. I also noted the DA's door was ajar.

I quickly slipped passed her desk and walked into the office. Before she could protest or stop me, the DA looked up from his desk and waved her off, as if saying not to worry, he'll take care of the intruder.

"I'm very sorry to bother you," I fumbled and saw his name on his desk, "ah, Mr. Williamson, but I have an urgent need for a small loan." Mr. Williamson didn't even blink an eye and calmly waited.

"I would like to hire you as my personal attorney while I'm in town, if it is at all possible. You see, my problem is that I happen to be the son of a wealthy man in Hong Kong. My father (*in heaven*) is processing the release of my trust fund for a substantial amount. It is being cleared for international exchange and should be transferred here shortly. I'm pressed for funds because I wish to purchase and open a Chinese restaurant in town. I'll need an attorney to handle a considerable amount of my trust, and also to guide me in being properly licensed and informed of the local ordinances for opening such an establishment."

I pulled out a fifty-dollar bill and laid it in front of him. "This is just a small advance bonus for your services. You'll be paid your fees accordingly. Would you do me the honor of being my counsel?" I graciously asked him.

Still calmly, although I did detect a twinkle of avarice, "Mr. Chung, it is I who would be honored to be of service to you. I see no conflict of interest as long as no city laws are breached on your part."

He stood up, put the fifty in his coat pocket, and extended a hand. "As of this hour, Mr. Chung, I am your legal representative and please feel free to call on me at any time." Mr. Williamson gave me his business card, and asked his secretary to come in. He introduced us and informed her to expect calls from his new client.

I shook his hand as I was leaving. I turned and said, "If you don't mind, Mr. Williamson, I've a small favor to ask of you. Would you kindly telephone to Dry Creek Savings and Loan, and say that you would vouch for a small loan of $3,000? No, better make it $5,000. I would be very grateful."

"Right away, Mr. Chung, it would be my pleasure," he smiled and nodded, pleased at the day's bonus.

I returned directly to the loan office. The manager was all smiles and had already prepared all the papers. He had a lovely stack of green money in front of him. I signed the papers and thanked him.

I walked out and went right next door to the cafe. "Well, howdy, partner," the surprised proprietor greeted me.

"Here's your $3,000 dollars cash." I returned his smile. "You can pick up your bait and tackle, 'cause you have all day to catch some big Missouri catfish."

He wasted no time. He picked up and counted the cash. Satisfied, he slapped the cafe keys on the counter, emptied the cash register, and gave me his dirty apron.

Without his hands, he moved the lit cigar from one side of his mouth to the other side, blew the smoke above my head, and said, "That's a mighty fair deal." He chewed his cigar, turned and spit bull's eye into the spittoon on the floor, and continued, "I know one thing sure 'bout a Chinaman—you can always trust their word on money matters."

I confess I was a bit shocked, witnessing myself doing this whole crazy act, but at the same time I was immensely enjoying it as a sort of spontaneous live theatre. I wondered how the last act of my insanity was to turn out. I suspected my soul had something to do with this. I had absolutely no idea what I was getting myself into.

As the smiling former proprietor, whose name I still did not know, headed for the front door, he turned saying; "By the way, Big Jim, da nigger cook, is OK and can be trusted, 'cept when he's skunk drunk 'bout every other day. Otherwise he makes an ass-kicking hot chilly-n-beans with biscuits and gravy. Well, I'll see y'all at the lake someday, fella. I reckon you'll be making chop suey! Don't mind if I try some when I drop by to see how yer doin! Good luck, y'all goin' to need lots of it." And he was out the door.

It was only two hours ago when I had come here for a 35-cent cup of coffee, and here I was—suddenly the new owner of this old, run-down dump of a cafe. I had a balance of $2,000 to run this business, pay the rent, and raise a family. I'd certainly created my own job.

It suddenly struck me what the true meaning of Kierkegaard's existential principle of the "Leap of Faith" really was. This was what I was doing—blindly jumping into a black hole of uncertainty to hopefully find the certainty within. I would need more than luck to pull this off.

I gave the place one passing glance and coughed. The once white walls had long since turned pale yellow and greasy, and the booths with torn, dirty coverings had the accumulated odor of smelly sweat from fat, gossipy ladies who salivated as they shoved lard-fried catfish from the lake the local kids used for skinny-dipping on hot summer moonlit nights.

I reached over and pulled on the half-torn seat cover and the rotten rag came off in my hand. I grabbed the cover and yanked. Underneath the cotton cushion was a solid oak, sawed-off church pew! I did the same to the other booths and discovered to my delight that all were the same beautiful oak. The place was filled with discarded church furniture. The counter was an old handmade tavern counter with its original brass foot railings, and behind it, three working soda faucets. There was also a large old jukebox filled with country westerns. I heard later that the former owner had bought the cafe from the original owner, a former Bible thumping itinerant preacher who gave sermons and sold dinners to his Jesus-screaming flock. It had been bought and converted into an ice cream parlor and café. It was known all around town for the best and largest banana splits for fifty-five cents and fresh-baked donuts for ten cents.

I thought I'd better hire the first person who walked in that day. A big fat white kid strolled in just then. "Hey, kid," I called, "you wanna job?" His eyes popped out and he nodded affirmative, too surprised for words to form in his blond crew cut head. He was a foot taller than I and sixteen years old.

"Answer this question, and I'll hire you right this second," I said. He nervously gulped. "What former president of the United States has his picture on this twenty-dollar bill, kid?" I asked him.

He shrugged and sadly shook his head. "Sorry, I don't know," and shamefully confessed that he had flunked mean ol' Miss Anderson's third grade class three times when he lived in Kirksville, Missouri.

I reached into my pocket and gave him a wrinkled twenty-dollar bill and showed him the picture. "Look-a-here, this honcho's name is Jackson and he's always on all the twenty-dollar bills floating around the whole U-Ass-of-A. Can you try to remember that?" He nodded with a big charming country bumpkin smile that made my day. That day, I had him memorize all the U.S. presidents on all the bills from Washington to Grant. When it came to cold hard cash, he was a darn fast learner, that fat *haoli* kid.

I gave him the twenty and told him to go across to Sherman's Paint Store and bring back three gallons of black paint, paint rollers, and brushes. When he returned I had poor drunk Jim, the cook, and the kid paint the whole place, ceiling and walls all black, including the booth walls, except the bench pews and counter. Any wood area I left unpainted.

By the second day I moved my personal things into my fresh, new, all-black establishment. I brought books by Sartre, Heidigger, Nietzsche, Boudelaire, Kierkegaard, Gurdjieff, Ouspenski, John Bennett, Henry Miller, and Alan Watts. I brought Zen books, the "I-Ching", Carl Jung, Kabbalistic and Sufi authors, T.S. Eliot, the Bible, the Qur'an, and dozens of other books with strange mystic tales not found even in the extensive university library at that time. I placed them in the huge front display window facing Broadway. I also brought the large oriental rug right off our living room floor, and some framed pictures and wall posters I had.

I could see that across the street, the corner tavern's owner and clientele were peering curiously, watching this bald-headed new foreigner working. No one knew what was to come.

My wife, Georgina, now using the name Bapak had given her, was elated and supportive. Although we were totally broke, which was our natural state, she had been content with our quiet, simple lifestyle at home. But now I was intent in following this spontaneous implosion that seemed to have thrust my life five years ahead of myself, to what was to be the end of the old and the beginning of the new.

Georgina artistically hand-painted our new name on the large glass window at the front of the cafe—the first psychodelic sign on Main Street USA.

INN OF THE DUBioUS (S)ELF
Wishes do come true (So Beware)

From inside the café the word "DUBioUS appeared as "SUBUD".

I brought porcelain tea containers, a case of vodka, cans of coffee, and other food supplies from home. Also, I brought my record collection, turntable, speakers, microphones, and bongo drums, and my new Wollensack tape recorder. I purchased all the latest top pop hits (of which I had been totally unaware for two years), jazz records, classics, a couple of operas, old folk songs, and early American ballads. There were some Indian Sitar records (Ravi Shankar), Buddy Holly, and of course, Elvis the King.

Most of the time in that cafe, I played my favorites—the country westerns from the cafe's dime-a-spin 45 rpm jukebox, which also had coin slots at the tables to punch in selections from the booths. I had Jim, the cook, and the kid, replace all the light bulbs with red, blue, and green spotlights. There were colored lights all around the windows. They both thought it funny that Chinese celebrated Xmas in late September, which I admit I led them to believe. After the black coffeehouse was decorated to my satisfaction, I turned on the main light with the large Chinese lantern cover, which I had sneaked from our rented home. The place really looked more like some old, tucked-away Chinese brothel and opium-smoking joint instead of the North Beach Bagel Shop I had tried to imitate.

I had no money left, even to run a weekend Grand Opening ad in the local Tribune. I was going to have to come up with a miracle to feed my little boys and their mother and pay the rent for the next two months. What to do?

I got it!

I hurriedly started using the public pay phone near the door. First I called Stephen's College Playhouse, then all the fraternity and sorority houses on every campus. I invited George C. Scott and all his students in acting classes, and told them to pass the word for free booze all weekend at the Grand Opening of my coffeehouse. I invited everyone to come-as-they-are, even in their pajamas, since Grand Opening would begin this Friday at midnight. Sunday's morning brunch would feature coffee, Mozart, and bagels, which in those days no one in Missouri had ever heard of.

Having lived and studied in Columbia before, I had made many friends south of Broadway, literally the other side of the railroad tracks. Fortunately, because of my color, I was permitted in both worlds. I contacted some buddies, some hot jazz musicians, poolroom and crap-shooting types, and their beautiful hot dancing ladies of the day and of the night. Many of them came to the grand opening.

Like two separate realities colliding, the whites and the blacks were being introduced to each other by a little bald headed cosmic elf. Total strangers, black and white met for the first time in their lives. It was scary and exciting to be sitting in the same booth. They crossed, mixed, merged, and fused into one human family. They were inter-exchanging, encountering, and sharing experiences of who they were in a jive-jumping, ass-kicking jamboree every weekend, and for shorter hours nightly. It was a brief, fleeting moment in history, like a temporary "time out zone" for those who happened to experience and share what it would be like to live together in one common human consciousness renaissance at the Inn of the DUBioUS (S)elf.

They all loved drinking my special oriental tea mixed with herbal spices, cinnamon, orange peelings, nutmeg, and vodka and eating my delicious home baked Chinese brownies and cookies with liberal sprinklings of marijuana whose pungent odor and smoke filled the Inn and drifted out into the streets. In those pre-hippie days, no one knew what that peculiar smell was, not even the cops. There were no laws against growing, harvesting, and smoking pot until much later.

Missourians had never before witnessed and heard loud, hearty, and giggling laughter coming from an all-night little tea house. How could it be possible that whites and Negroes would dare hold hands and laugh and have fun in Protestant America in broad daylight on Main Street, USA?

There was a large basement under the Inn for storing supplies and junk. I cleaned, scrubbed, and painted the whole basement to make myself a special private room to perform my latihan uninterrupted. Since the den of iniquity was in session above, I figured it would be best to do the latihan beneath so as to divert the dark spirits.

Before long, several friends I had made were becoming curious about what I was doing in the basement alone at all hours. Soon I spread the contact and there were now eight or ten others who joined me in practicing the latihan.

I began noticing many unusual phenomena. When the activity upstairs got wilder, the latihan would change course as though paralleling the people's feelings upstairs. I found myself screaming louder and louder and acting increasingly crazy in my basement. With the din going on upstairs, no one could hear the madness below. It was so strong and intense, I would scream loud obscenities, bang more furiously against the supply boxes, and smash and throw things around. I sometimes wept so profoundly as to make me question again—what *is* this, and where am I heading with this mysterious contact? Am I actually turning toward my dark side and promoting evil with this Inn of the DUBioUS (S)elf?

Another change seemed to come over my closest friends, those whom I had met when the Inn first opened. They had been as wild as the newcomers were later, but as these regulars would always sit in my favorite booth at the back, whether I was there or not, they became my closest friends. Their wild behavior seemed to have subsided considerably. Many times I would simply sit and watch quietly. When I did appear, I would find my booth filled with the same batch sitting quietly, watching the others or reading!

Both men and women student regulars began assisting spontaneously with the welcoming and caring of the newcomers. They introduced them to others, as I had been doing from the start, and helped them make new friends, particularly those of different races, sex, and interests.

I was fully aware that people were not coming for great food—for there was none, except coffee and cakes, which vanished rapidly. Nor was it free alcohol, which was only available during the grand opening. By then I was broke. But they were packing the place, looking for something to nourish and feed an inner hunger. They were delightfully surprised to find others of similar interests and concerns and to find that they were not alone in their spiritual hunger.

My young clientele all reminded me of that young lonely seeker of 1950, Tien-Yau, the wild bohemian. But now at least they had what I didn't have back then—an open, free place to hang out in and share with each other, a place to call home for their young spirits.

Sam-Tio recognized, understood, and accepted all who came. Sam-Tio was always there. He often even chose to stay at the Inn all night rather than go home, astonished and delighted with the spontaneous surprises that were occurring every day.

At first the connection did not occur to me consciously. It sneaked into my consciousness that I, Tien-Yau, was now being introduced to his identical twin, his human soul. Tien-Yau would not have dared or even been able to conceive and open such a crazy and absurd coffeehouse. It was Sam-Tio Chung who gave extemporaneous talks, standing on the counter with the mike, to the sardine-packed customers who demanded to hear more and more of the strange and hilarious tales of his life.

Tien-Yau would have shied away from all that open affection and interaction. However, Sam-Tio could not be restrained and had to be let free. He felt the feelings of all who came near him. And he loved them all.

Something was beginning to happen. I just let it go and observed whatever occurred without interrupting, simply watching and going along with where this mysterious force was taking me.

The Inn of the DUBioUS (S)elf became the first racially integrated existentialist coffeehouse west of the Mississippi and east of San Francisco. It was smack in the middle of a college town of 30,000 souls, where it became an overnight smash hit. The house was fully packed within the first week of its opening. It would be another five to ten years before the civil rights movement swept the nation by storm. The Inn was an early experimental training ground for recruiting young students; men and women warriors for the great civil rights battle to come.

There were elements in the town who hated my establishment. They wanted this interracial blemish shut down. The police made frequent raids to check on whether the Inn could be closed for some infraction, always unsuccessfully.

Finally, I was put in jail. The cops stopped me and found that I was still driving with a California driver's license—not having gotten the required Missouri driver's license within 10 days of my Missouri residency. At the coffeehouse, the college girls helped out by working as waitresses while raising money to get me out of jail. When they came with the bond money, I said I wouldn't leave until the girl in the next cell, a beautiful young black woman in her thirties, was also bailed out. So the college students went back to the coffee house and raised more bail money for my new friend. She didn't have any place to stay, so I let her stay in the basement of the Inn and went home to my family. I got an urgent call later that evening, or rather early the next morning to come to the coffeehouse. As I drove up, I was shocked—I had never seen so many cars parked outside the establishment. People, three deep, were lined up outside peering through the windows because there was no room inside. Loud singing and thumping could be heard from outside. I squeezed myself through the crowd and there was my jail mate in the middle of the floor, stripped nude and dancing wildly to bongo drums and the stomping and chanting crowds of black and white patrons. She turned everyone on. Blacks and whites joined in, dancing with a new freedom and openness never seen in the Dixieland.

Folks came from as far north as Chicago, as far south as New Orleans, from St. Louis and the outskirts of the great slaughterhouses of Topeka and Kansas City. The Inn was to become a real underground of early civil rights consciousness, preceding the campus riots and Mississippi racial riots, with nightly bongo drums and jazz, black and whites dancing and kissing in public, police raids, 35-cent marijuana joints, and other outrageous human events.

Perhaps an alien UFO from some other world, the spirit of the Inn, appeared in broad daylight, circled the Midwestern town, stopped and silently fired some kind of laser beam on a corner cafe below and then, as suddenly as it appeared, it zoomed away, leaving a trail of aromatic marijuana smoke.

After less than six months of its brief life, the Inn of the DUBioUS (S)elf vanished over the horizon's edge. Years later, its legend was still whispered in the halls of academia, as the most astounding sight this town had ever experienced. It is rumored that from the Inn, many of the young college kids went to California where some joined a mystic movement of unknown origin. Other native folks swear that innocent white college girls were either brainwashed or abducted, or both, by a bald headed, slant-eyed, soya-eating Eastern guru, most likely taken to Tibet by that one-legged elf.

From the moment I arrived back in Columbia, life had become an incredible trip. I had never even imagined or considered that life could be one long continuous circus until everything started happening on its own.

Something was released in the Inn. I knew and could feel the impact it was having on the entire town. Many hated the Inn, while many others loved it. But, although the Inn of the DUBioUS (S)elf was a shamelessly smashing success, it was an abominable financial disaster. As in the joke, the operation was highly successful, but unfortunately the patient died before he could appreciate the brilliance of the new surgical technique.

Meanwhile, I had been carrying a heavy graduate load of courses in abnormal psychology, statistics, diagnostics, and a course in Freud's psychoanalysis and interpretation of dreams. The latter course was with my favorite professor Dr. David Bakan, a Freudian scholar who read chapters of a book he was writing, "Freud and Jewish Mysticism" to his class for feedback.

We became close friends and David invited me to his home for hot meals and long discussions. Dave had all his students sleep with pencil and paper next to their beds nightly to record our dreams upon awakening. We then read our dreams aloud and the dream seminar students would practice Freud's dream analysis. It was the most memorable class I ever had in all my years of university life. Dave was invited to join the faculty of the University of Chicago around that time (and later, Harvard). So in addition to the impending loss of the coffeehouse, I was to lose my best friend.

The Asylum

As Tien-Yau, I was desperately in need of a real job with a regular weekly or monthly paycheck—money to keep family and self alive. But of course, my soul, Sam-Tio was not in the least concerned or worried about his twin brother, who was still ruled by space and time. Within his cocoon, Tien-Yau had undergone a transformation. And now a miracle caused something to go backwards in time, resulting in a role reversal; Tien-Yau was now the entity within someone named Sam-Tio who moved spontaneously and free in real life and time, using Tien-Yau's body to do as commanded.

Dr. Burt Wallenstein, who was the same age as me, was one of my best friends in the inner circle of the Do-Nothing student group and an Assistant Professor of Psychology at the University. He was a part-time staff member in the maximum security state mental hospital and its special unit for the criminally insane. The asylum was in an old three-story building, totally self-supported with its own large dairy farm, vegetable garden, water tower, and generator.

Burt had earlier bugged me to work at the asylum, but I constantly turned him down. Tien-Yau had no burning desire to work in an imperial palace of the insane. But due to the inn's imminent bankruptcy, I had no other option, so I applied. I secretly hoped to be rejected.

A few days later, Burt came to my house early in the morning. "Aren't you ready?" Burt asked as I opened the door in my briefs. "We're already late for the staff meeting!"

Noticing the puzzlement on my sleepy face, he asked, "Don't tell me you forgot about our appointment for Monday?"

I had absolutely no recall of having promised Burt anything. Suddenly, it occurred to me, Sam-Tio must have agreed with Burt about something. Yes, it was Sam-Tio who had agreed to the Monday appointment at the asylum.

In spite of, or perhaps because of such schizophrenic tendencies, after a preliminary and unscheduled introduction to Burt's staff friend Dr. Kenneth Sommers, the hospital hired me before I had even filled in the application for employment! Dr. Sommers warmly shook my hand and said he had immensely enjoyed being in my coffeehouse. Burt had taken him a couple of times to my establishment and told him all about me. Before the week was up, many other staff members had welcomed me with equal enthusiasm. Many had either visited or heard wild rumors about the Inn.

Ken showed me my office. It had a desk and three other chairs. I stared at the objects hanging behind the desk, a pair of handcuffs, a club, and a white canvas jacket. "Interesting décor," pointing out the objects to Ken as if I knew what they were for. My strategy in any unfamiliar place was to remain cool, unconcerned, and matter of fact, even though my legs trembled and my heart jumped and got tangled up with my speechless tongue. I hoped to seem tough, detached, and not easily conned or frightened by anything or anyone. I've been told many times that I should have gone into acting.

Fortunately, I'm a quick learner and *ad lib* faker. At least, I thought to myself, it must be impossible to be fired from a state asylum, unless you were madder than the inmates.

After less than an hour of orientation and talk about my responsibilities with my new boss, Ken, I was immediately sent to the front lines—that tiny empty sterile office.

My job was to interview and fill out the data sheets on all new admissions as they came in that day or night. I was quickly moved to night shift, except weekends when I ran the Inn. I was not informed, but discovered before the end of the first day, that the newly admitted were often accompanied by the police, county sheriffs, or armed task force. They were violent, under special observation, or just plain regular killers. Now I knew why my office had those cute objects. The white canvas was a straight jacket. I tested them all. It gave me my first experience of what impotence felt like.

The other part of my job was to do a case write-up of the basic data and description of the incident that brought them here, the social background, and any observable unusual behavior of the new admittees. Further, I was to read all my write-ups to the diagnostic staff the following Monday. All the department heads of the hospital convened to decide the new patient's diagnosis, treatment, and ward placement. I had to have all the write-ups ready to turn in to Ken for correction by 9 am every Friday. Later I was assigned to the back wards of long term schizophrenics. My job there was to select, do therapy, and prepare inmates for probationary discharge and possible job placement in the community outside the hospital.

It was one thing for me to have studied psychology in my undergraduate years. It was an entirely different experience to breathe the reality of the mentally afflicted as-it-really-is. Their sufferings haunted and plagued my screaming nightly dreams. The peculiar odors of the terror-stricken schizophrenics and the rank cancerous unloved, the psychotics with abandoned lonely hearts, and the geriatric wards were worlds apart and totally distinct from each other. I quickly began to smell their differences, distinctly different again from the evil, cunning, scummy sweat of the criminally insane who were housed on a separate campus in a high security, barb-wired enclosure, each locked in a separate prison cell. But the most painful and tragic were the severely disturbed children and teenagers from dysfunctional, alcoholic, or abusive families.

Every day I thought about quitting and walking out of this inhuman hell. After some time, patiently performing my initial duties, I still did not know why or for what possible meaning or purpose I was sentenced to experience this asylum of humanity. So I did a latihan there. As the latihan subsided, I feebly washed my face in the bowl of holy water near the door of the small prayer room that was open to anyone in the hospital. I returned to the small admission office of the large state hospital to find two armed uniformed policemen holding a handcuffed patient between them. The newly admitted was later brought into the diagnostic staff meeting after I read the case history write up. This was my first internship assignment for Ph.D. studies as a rehabilitation psychologist.

Upon returning home from the state mental hospital early that morning I swore not to celebrate Christmas this year, except for our two children. I would bring presents to the hospital and help the staff deck the halls of madness with flashing merry lights and fill the air with choral singing, and try to untie the straightjackets of my newly adopted humanity. I had been the founder and sole member of my own Club Asylum for so long, it was nice to have friends who knew how to not disturb other's madness, and stick with their own insanity. I continued my latihans in the hospital prayer room.

The more I did the latihan, the more the madhouse of my sentence in hell changed. It reversed rapidly many times over. The asylum became my Ph.D. candidacy in spiritual advocacy, the secret training school for disciples in the helping arts. It was here, via the latihan contact, that I was being mentored in the new spiritual psychology of man through my own experiences, not the academic psychology classes that I often skipped. I never even bought those unbearably heavy textbooks. Somehow, I always managed to score high on tests without studying. I never gave a damn for most of what was being taught, if it didn't confirm what reality was teaching me.

The helping profession, I quickly discovered, is the most difficult work of any profession I know. It was in the madhouse that I learned how to be an unbiased loving compassionate human being. The patients taught me how to respond with real love and caring. I began to develop a high respect for some of the true helping warriors among these mental health workers. The burnout rate—psychiatrists have one of the highest suicide rates—is high because of all the acute suffering one absorbs into one's spirit. Tien-Yau Chung could handle only so much, but Sam-Tio was a constant and incredible amazement in his wide capacity to absorb the suffering around him. If he was open and loving at the Inn of the Dubious (S)elf, he was even more so in the asylum of the hopeless and tragically insane.

During the next three years, I remained in the asylum to see how I could help to alleviate at least a portion of the unimaginable horrors of their insanity. How hot the heat can be in this pit, is beyond description. Had I not, as Tien-Yau, pleaded and yearned to have been born in the millennium when giants and prophets had walked the earth; that I might *personally* experience what the early disciples had undergone as they followed God's prophets and messengers as spiritual warriors who waged battle against the forces of evil? It is often said, don't ask for something if you are not really ready to handle it. Later, I had this gut wrenching feeling that I might have bitten off more than I could chew.

I could tell when the weekends began and the national holidays were approaching. On these nights the halls of insanity were suddenly packed with new admittees. It was a week before Xmas when I was transferred to the owl shift from 11 pm to 7 am. Before I could even finish with one client, another was already being pushed into my cubbyhole office, barren except for the witchdoctor's tools on the wall.

The psychology department of the hospital needed someone to work in the criminally insane group, so Bert suggested that I be transferred there.

My First Meeting with a
Criminally Insane Patient

My first criminally insane patient was Gregory; "a young, single, white male of 28 years", is how I began writing his case history. Only this time I was treating him and not just writing his history. Gregory had volunteered to be my weekly patient. Up until now, I had read too many patient files and was sick of just reading and not working with them.

I didn't pull out or read Gregory's file. Without telling my superiors or anyone else, I wanted to experience what old Father Sigmund Solomon Freud had first experienced with his first patient ("Solomon" was Freud's secret Jewish family nickname). Freud had no training, no case history file, no formal tutorial about how it was to meet a total stranger in a one-to-one direct encounter without any prior knowledge and information. I knew about this when interviewing new admissions, but not in the treatment process.

The security guard asked if I needed his presence with Gregory, which is customary in most cases. I declined, and thanked him. He was pleased to have a long coffee break. I took a deep breath and hoped the latihan contact did not abandon me. I remained quiet for a couple of minutes.

The guard ushered Gregory into my redecorated office, which had formerly been one of the cells, the toilet conveniently behind my desk and still functional. I quickly hid Freud's *Interpretation of Dreams* under some other papers on my desk.

"Hi doc," Gregory gave a pleasant smile, "Most people call me Greg, and you must be... ?"

"Sam-Tio Chung, but call me Sam," I shook his hand, "It's simple and easier."

He pulled up the chair and sat casually, brushing his hospital-issue blue jeans carefully, though they were clean and recently pressed. "You must be still working on your Ph.D. and doing your internship, Mr. Chung?" He spoke clearly and succinctly in the soft gentle voice of a young southern gentleman of breeding and unpretentious perspicuity.

I could not help being instantly charmed by such a handsome, intelligent young fellow. I felt my legs tense under the desk and felt beads of nervous perspiration under my tight collar, so with practiced casualness, loosened my tie.

"So, Greg, how've they been treating you?" I fidgeted with my tie.

"I don't think you really want to know, Mr. Chung. But, all things considered, I suppose fair to middlin', as the folks down here like to say."

I don't know why, but I blushed and tried to hide it.

He chuckled, "Excuse me, but I can't help but notice your nervous embarrassment." He continued, "Look, Mr. Chung, I know how difficult and baffling it must be to have your first real patient to treat. No, no, please, you needn't deny it. Besides, there's nothing to be ashamed about. It's only natural to be intimidated and scared the first time at anything. Though it may be a disadvantage to you, I have thousands of hours of every known therapeutic method tried on me, by the top doctors in the country."

Greg actually made me relax, and I began to feel safe and trusting. "Obviously, Mr. Chung, you haven't read my voluminous file yet? I commend you on your bravery, though I would not recommend you do the same with some of the other dangerous gooney birds in here."

It flashed through my mind, *I'll have to do some creative reporting of my session today. I'll be damned if I'm going to write the real truth of what's taking place. If they found out the truth, I would top this madhouse history for being the dumbest Chinaman between the Mississippi River and China's Great Wall. I will use every ounce of will power to suppress this meeting.*

Again, with his sweet blue smiling eyes, Greg said off-handedly, "Mr. Chung, you needn't worry, our confidentiality is locked in this room. In fact, I have taken a liking to you. You're easy to trust, because it is difficult for you to not be genuinely open."

All right, I thought to myself, *this is just not working out like the books said. He has turned the tables on me. I like him, but I'm the staff around here. I should do something about this and take control. But I can't. And I don't like it one bit when I feel this impotent. I won't be able to talk to anyone about this, not even Burt, my most trusted friend. What's next? Is this whiz kid setting me up to cry next? I better find a good excuse to terminate and split.*

"Greg, I'm terribly sorry, but I forgot all about the 11 am staff meeting. Do you mind if we postpone our session to Friday same time?"

"Did I do something wrong, Mr. Chung?" he asked. "Please forgive me if I have in some way breached."

"No, no, don't be absurd, Greg. Listen, Friday, OK?" I banged the door for the guard to let me out from my own office cell. From the corner of my eye I still saw the puzzled look on Greg's face.

"Was everything all right, Mr. Chung?" the guard questioned my short visit. I assured him all went well, and I was late for a staff meeting.

More Asylum Latihans

During my 4 am breaks, I would go to the empty hospital chapel. No sooner did the door close, than the latihan threw me flat down on the cold floor. So that I would not alert anyone, I muffled my screams with my rolled up white frock with the invisible blood of the insane smeared on it. My sobbing, thrashing, and coughing had no ending or beginning. It came like a flash flood on a desert night. I raised my head off the floor and my teary eyes happened to catch the eye of the crucified one on his cross in that semi-dark chapel. My God, is this how that poor fellow felt? Instead of giving me any relief, the half-nude figure on the cross only increased the agony I felt.

I held my head in both hands to hold my brains from coming out of my ears. Next door to the chapel was the detox section. Their forlorn cries for mercy merged with the tortured, high-pitched singing of my latihan. I felt like a wandering infant lost among the world's damned. What were my sins and the sins I inherited from ancient Cathay that fated me to be in this hellhole?

The world seems to have changed dramatically for the worse since that man on the cross last came. In the name of God—*why*?

I Discover Psychodrama

I had decided to cut through the main patient recreation and visiting room and get myself a soda. It was a large room where many patients, visitors, guest, and staff congregated, the town's water hole, where one could not tell who was and was not committed, especially without the midsize white frocks. My own oversize frock dragged the ground, making me look like "Sweet Pea" in Popeye, and my long sleeves constantly unfolded, covering my hands.

Without looking, I sat in the first empty chair, relieved to escape. I took a couple of big gulps from the ice-cold soda bottle. Someone asked for a cigarette. I reached inside my shirt pocket for my pack of Lucky Strikes, offered him one and put one in my mouth. He leaned over and lit mine. "Mind if I sit here?" he asked. I shook my head in the negative and gestured that he was welcome.

I had still not paid any attention to my surroundings. The place was, as usual, filled with smoke and a chattering crowd of people in long pajamas, jeans, gowns, frocks, suits, dresses, and the overalls that many long-confined patients preferred. How unlike their former homes in the surrounding lush farms and dairy lands, fluffy new winter snow sprinkled like tiny white carnations covering the land of the great Midwest.

Suddenly, my attention went to four individuals who were arguing and screaming at each other. I couldn't figure out what the commotion was all about. One plainly clothed young man was talking behind a patient, while a young female intern scolded the patient, as if she were his mother. The man behind the patient must have been whispering in his ear, "What's going on, Jack, say what you're feeling and no bullshit."

Another man pulled up a chair near the young female who quickly turned around and snapped angrily at him. "Is that all you're going to do about your son?" she screeched.

Suddenly, the patient burst into tears, weeping, his body trembling. Everyone circled and huddled around the weeping patient, their hands on his head and shoulders. They began rocking him back and forth, some actually crying, most with their heads bowed. Then they scattered. The same young man, the leader, I surmised, called, "OK, very good. See y'all next week, same time. Then he turned to the crying patient, "Jack, come with us."

I realized that an hour had passed. I had been totally transfixed as I witnessed this most astonishing scene.

A strange feeling had enveloped me, as if I were in the center of a serious dialogue with strangers. Something fascinating clicked deep inside me. The blood sped wildly through my brain and my heart raced as if struck by a powerful lightning bolt. It was like falling in love for the first time! A deep excited feeling was surging through my body. I felt like a treasure hunter striking gold, but one who had never seen what gold looked like raw, from the primeval earth. It was like suddenly being awakened in the middle of the night by a familiar voice, only to realize I was talking in my sleep. I heard the voice say loudly, *this is your moment, seize it now!*

Just then I happened to spot my friend Burt talking with one of the pretty young female interns. Burt saw me and called, "Hey, Sam, come here!"

I went up to them and Burt introduced us. We nodded that we had met at a staff meeting. "Hey," Burt stood, "Jimmy's gonna do his feedback circle. Come on, Sam, join us." We followed and I sat in the back row behind the circle of people.

By the end of the feedback session, I learned that staff volunteers ran these weekly groups and that next meeting was to be their last. I had Burt introduce me to their leader and I heard a few words and a name: Dr. Jacob L. Moreno, founder of the Academy of Psychodrama and Group Psychotherapy in Beacon, New York. I wrote the address down.

I went home to think about it. The experience of seeing the psychodrama in the patient's canteen was so vividly my moment of truth that I decided to do a latihan test, Subud-style. Bapak had tested many fascinating questions with us in San Francisco by asking us to receive in our latihans the truth of this or that. He used it to help us experience that each of us had an inner knowing beyond any thinking, emotion, teacher, or teachings. I needed to know from testing if psychodrama was in line with my soul's true destiny. I went home and did my first real test alone.

My receiving was, in short—go for it! I was so stunned that I tested the question twice more, each time receiving a clear "yes." So I returned to the hospital and submitted my resignation, effective immediately.

With Dr. Moreno in New York

The next thing I knew, I was aboard a flight for New York City! I was about to enter orbit around a living legend, with whom I was going to spend the next few weeks in private training. Dr. Jacob L. Moreno, a psychiatrist from Vienna and a contemporary of Sigmund Freud himself, had established his Academy in upstate New York, in a town aptly named Beacon.

The New York cab driver dropped me at the gate of an immense, green-pastured estate with several large buildings and many smaller cottages. A lovely lady in her mid-thirties, Zerka, the wife of Dr. Moreno greeted me warmly. Immediately, with my luggage still in my hands, I followed her into a large theatre. A small group was sitting on the lower stage step, listening to a large overweight man in his late sixties with a massive head and deep dark eyes that looked straight through you.

Moreno spoke with both hands punctuating and waving like an opera conductor. His phrases soared and paused in mid-air suspension, then suddenly looped through another phrase with a slight tilt of his noble Roman nose. While his fearsome eagle eyes peered from beneath their dark caverns, his singular passion driven heat missile launched from his fingertips and detonated on impact in my hungry brain. It caused such an implosion that I had to close my eyes to shield myself from the blinding brilliance. I could feel only ecstatic screaming pain, a virginal yin mind impregnated by a giant yang sperm, the sexuality of fresh new Chi-energized conceptualization exploding and flooding all the zillions of my cerebral cells into a terrifying chaotic neural burnout. Then utter silence.

The sound of one hand clapping was then ignited by Moreno's magic—awakening and igniting the long-buried, sleeping, unanswerable *koan* within me. The radioactive white light of understanding rained down and soaked the parched, dry land of my being, and a sudden flowering of fragrant meanings perfumed the path of Sam-Tio's destiny.

Moreno was my first real intellectual encounter with a legendary genius and guru. I had always wanted such an encounter, wanted to share unabashedly my stuffed portfolio of suspended questions with a live guru. His gifted madness seemed to engulf me in insane laughter, soaring me upwards to actually sit at the council table of great master giants who played conundrum chess just to tease and checkmate fools, such as I, with their twinkling brilliance.

There was an unquestioning acceptance of who and what I was, as though I were a favorite adopted child-giant who needed firm, but gentle discipline.

There were about seven of us that remained throughout his intensive seminar. It was his custom to have all his students attend meals at his table at home, a few yards away from his private theatre. At his insistence, I had to sit right next to him. As always, I assumed that my late arrival made me the densest of all and therefore needed remedial tutoring. The other students were all practicing psychiatrists, psychologists, psychiatric social workers, or other impressive professionals. On weekends other notable visitors, such as heads of clinics or chiefs of university departments, came from all over the USA and Europe for intensive crash courses.

Each seminar student had his day on center stage, all day and sometimes part of the night! Moreno talked, observed, paused, and sometimes suddenly leaped, moving behind his subject, going off stage laughing and pointing, waving his hands, all the while his sharp cunning missing nothing. He never missed the whispering of other students who were watching and giggling at the poor victim in the center. In an instant, he would surprise the gigglers by zeroing in with a stunning, off-the-cuff insight, piercing their secret thoughts.

In a flash he would vanish and reappear, looming twelve feet tall in awesome deep rage, acting the part of the angry father, hated and feared employer, wrathful devil, or vengeful dead spirit. He was a consummate actor of all roles. He was the master charmer, the director without a script who created imaginary brick walls, rooms and castles, only to give chase and play hide-and-seek with buried fears and hatreds.

He could rip asunder iron-door defenses, leaving the protagonist naked as the day he or she was born. Yet Moreno could be suddenly tender and understanding, gently wiping away the tears of raw, exposed psyches, as the person was cuddled and rocked in his huge warm arms. But only if the protagonist's honesty was authentic and true.

Zerka, Moreno's wife and associate, was the embodiment of Moreno's dynamic *femme fatale.* Zerka was the first woman I had ever met who had all her remarkable qualities, talents and gifts, not as dormant possibilities but in all their fully developed manifest power. She was a most incredible woman, who came closest to my ideal fantasy of an equal working mate. Like the eagle's mate, Zerka had all the cunning and speed of insight to tease, flush out, divert, guide, and entrap her victim for her mate's final kill.

Their teamwork was a ballet of perfect precision and timing. It was a purely improvisational and unrehearsed choreography, with no verbal instructions or dialogue. Only keen senses could detect the swift, silent, dolphin communications between them. At times, like some male and female mammals, it was difficult to distinguish who was who in their quick reversals and switching of roles.

Their impact was unfailingly on the mark, and the subject's moment of truth emerged from its devastated defensive fortress. One's soul emerged from the debris, exposing hidden tunnels of repressed and suppressed self-denials, façades of shielded guilt cracked wide open and ready for reprogramming or psycho-surgical correction.

Unlike those who loved their own diplomas above all and forever reminded everyone of their all-knowingness, Moreno was simply unique. What each saw in Moreno was, in most cases, his own projection and wish reflected larger than life. His laughter would ring like a delighted child when someone's precious ego tumbled down from the high lofty wall of pride. After dinner, Moreno talked and answered everyone's questions until midnight. I had many questions, but I wanted instead to silently use the latihan to absorb all and everything about Moreno and his whole magical world, so I remained silent.

Having this contact for almost two years now, I thought it might be as good a time as any to use the latihan testing to evaluate my place here with Dr. Moreno and the reality behind his practice of psychodrama.

....body begins some slight swaying motions, head turning, neck relaxing, legs, hips, and chest rock and sway in slow rhythmic motions, as both arms begin extending outward, moving back and forth across the chest and then extending like flower pedals opening, half-shutting, then opening again....entire body now moves effortlessly in harmonic motion. There is a slow stretching of all limbs and joints.

Chung:	*"Hello, Are you present, Sam-Tio?"*
Sam-Tio:	*"Hi, Chung, I've been waiting for you. Your vibes are clear, over!"*
Chung:	*"Feels great! Love you Sam."*
Sam-Tio:	*"Ditto five times."*
Chung:	*"How did you feel about the day's events?"*
Sam-Tio:	*"Interesting, brother."*
Chung:	*"Just interesting?"*
Sam-Tio:	*"What meaning do you wish to focus on?"*
Chung:	*"Hmmm…." (Reflecting on the questions to ask. Both are silent).*
Sam-Tio:	*"What is the meaning and purpose of being present with Moreno's training?"*

Chung's body begins to sway and rock, moving in a slow dance. He feels distinctly Sam-Tio's presence throughout his entire body. His head is clear. His heart is ready to receive. He experiences the entity within, which is Sam-Tio, the soul of Chung. It is like meeting an old friend this time, one having a real existence able to relate and respond to Chung.

Sam-Tio, his soul, moves silently about the cottage, then outside to the fresh cut grass, as the moon slips behind the night clouds. He meanders, then enters Moreno's theatre, gliding down the middle aisle and up on to the stage. He stands on the presidium's edge, looking all around. In one huge absorption, Sam-Tio takes into his system all the vibes in the theatre. Sam-Tio calls forth all the spirits in the theatre from Moreno's early days until to the present. The spirits come and relate all that has gone on in this place. Sam-Tio's feelings experience all the scenes and the emotions of all those who have occupied these theatre seats, all the spirits and ghosts of the participants.

Sam-Tio is moving all over the stage in a rhythmic Tai Chi dance movement, his arms and hands and legs swaying, leaping, and flying across the stage. He flies up to the ceiling to examine the spotlights, then looks at the rows and rows of theatre seats, then moves downward, circling round and round like a slowly twirling Sufi.

Sam-Tio absorbs so many different emotions—tears and memories, infancy through manhood, blocked feelings, cold painful agonies and cries for help, all ranges of emotions. Sam absorbs and absorbs in the theatre. He absorbs images of people in conflict, conflict among families, *"No, no, no PLEASE, dad,*

PLEASE mom… don't fight, PLEASE… it HURTS!" and on and on and on. The different ghosts and different strange spirits, good and evil, all move in and out, back and forth, in anger, sadness, and confusion. Sam absorbs and absorbs, inhaling everything into his being, while singing his song of release, soothing and calming the spirit's anxieties in that theatre. Sam-Tio nods his head, speaking without words to the spirits, telling them silently, "It's all right, its all right now."

Dr. Moreno took me with him to his New York City Friday night Theatre of the Spontaneous, giving me the chance to direct psychodrama there. He asked if I was interested in staying on in New York and if so, invited me to become the director of his theatre in New York. I thanked him and told him I was very honored to be offered this position, but that I needed to return to complete my doctoral studies.

Back to the Asylum

I had always admired and wished I were an artist but I had yet to find a medium. So I decided to live my life as an art form by living spontaneously, with a passion for adventure and discovery. I sailed around and explored the inner universe of my being, living and acting it out on my life's stage.

I discovered I could transform psychodrama to become my art form. I had already found that the fifty-minute therapeutic hour was ineffective. It took at least ten to fifteen minutes to "warm up" and then in the midst of something meaningful—time to stop. Only by doing one and a half to two hour sessions was is it possible to get anywhere productive. I learned in private practice that the time allotted had nothing to do with therapeutic efficacy, but rather money—the pragmatics of fees. The therapist can see one more client per day with the fifty-minute hour.

When I returned from the intensive with Moreno, I was accepted back to my job at the Missouri asylum. Since no one was supervising me, I could spend all day with one patient if I wanted. My superior was a TB specialist from Argentina, Dr. Gonzales. Many government mental hospitals hired foreign MDs with no psychiatric training. Dr. Gonzales gave me total authority to do whatever I wanted. I wrote prescriptions for drugs the patients needed and slipped them under the door for his signature. Only one thing was expected of me—if anyone asked for him, I was to say that he was not in and take a message. I, and no one else, could disturb him. He then locked himself in his office and watched TV or read his Life, Time, and other magazines all day.

I spent whole days creating and experimenting with the patients and the groups I put together. In most cases, I spent all day with either one patient or with a group. Aside from Moreno's at the VA hospital in Washington, DC, I started the first full-blown psychodrama theatre in any state mental hospital between Washington DC and California.

I found I could make the group more interesting and dynamic if I added hospital attendants who usually had nothing otherwise to do but watch TV. I invited pretty college girls to my "crazies" sessions, in order to stir up the patient's schizophrenic hallucinations. This cut through the passive thorazine stupor—the patients became animated and alive. I created what was undoubtedly the wildest and freest psychodrama theatre at that time. I must thank those beautiful, mad people for really teaching me how to deal with insanity. Some dimensions of insanity only appear crazy in the eyes of a beholder who is not familiar with, or may be threatened by the primordial rawness of the truth expressed by the insane.

One day I went into the local bowling alley to buy a pack of cigarettes. I heard the owner complaining to a patron that he was going to close on Mondays because business was terribly slow.

I turned and said, "Excuse me, I have suggestion how you can get a big free advertisement in the newspaper."

He turned and looked at me curiously, "So, how would you do that?"

"Let me bring my patients from the mental hospital to bowl next Monday, and I will call the newspaper about a special event to cover, like 'The Monday Night Mad Bowlers' for a headline special with photos."

The proprietor was excited, "You got yourself a deal, how's next Monday?"

The following Monday morning I drove the big yellow state mental hospital bus, with fifty laughing and screaming schizophrenics who waved at shocked pedestrians as we drove through the center of town. They were dressed in their usual hospital suspender overalls. They were referred to as the "back ward" schizophrenic patients because most had been locked in the back wards of the hospital for ten, fifteen, and more years. This group had been part of a first of its kind rehab project that I had created to give training to these patients so they could reenter into the community. This field trip appealed to the hospital superintendent because it could be included into a pending federal grant application for rehabilitation of the mentally ill.

We pulled into the bowling alley parking lot. The patients hip-hopped, giggled, and skipped in excitement, in contrast to their normal state of being very subdued from the medications they took.

I told them they could all have an ice cream cone at the soda fountain. Watching them laughing and jumping as they licked their ice cream cones, ice cream dripping down their cheeks, was a sight to behold. I couldn't help but fall in love with these innocent souls. I saw them not as inmates of a mental hospital but rather as childlike human beings. My love for them opened a channel in my heart to work with these people.

The owner greeted us warmly and shook hands with the many patients who offered their hands. He demonstrated bowling instructions and had his assistants help put bowling shoes on the patients. Then they picked up the bowling balls and began bowling. All the balls rolled down the gutters, some bouncing over into the next lane. One patient bent over and pushed the ball between his legs like a football center player. Another stood in the middle of the lane as a human pin, waiting to be hit by the ball.

I gave some change to one of them to play the jukebox. A jumping country western song came blaring into the bowling alley. Two of the assistants brought the hot dogs and sodas I had ordered for all of them.

Everyone had a grand time. The following day the story and pictures were in the newspaper.

The Psychodrama
of the Criminally Insane

My first psychodrama patient after returning from Moreno's institute was actually the same Gregory in the criminally insane section of the asylum. I had left for New York feeling completely unprepared to deal with his insidiously clever façade. Now I gathered together about five other criminally insane patients in this section to create the first therapy group in my psychodrama theatre. I got permission to use the cafeteria to run the groups.

I began by asking Gregory to act out the psychodrama of his parents. His father was a severe and demanding minister of his church. There was a significant other character, the Deacon, an old man who had worked with his father for years. When it came time to get a volunteer to play the Deacon, none of the patients wanted to play the role—so I did. We ended up on the floor in a simulated fight in the "church basement" where there was a small workshop filled with tools. Gregory, at fifteen years of age, hated the Deacon for having been molested by him for years.

Gregory was sitting straddled on my stomach as I lay on the floor. He froze and started to shake and perspire. His eyes opened wide and I could feel the terror of a hidden beast in him arising, but was severely blocked. He pinned me down with his weight, holding one of my arms under his knee.

I could feel the terrible fear and rage in my own chest, but I instinctively reacted as if I were the old Deacon, filled with humiliation there on the floor, because this kid wasn't putting out like he had done so meekly many times before. So I screamed angrily and with mocking derision, "Get the fuck off me, Greg."

Greg: (he trembles as if about to go into a seizure.) "I'll…I'll…"

(The whole group backs away from the scene. The attendant comes forward, but I wave him off. This is the red light that stops most all professionals—if they are smart and cautious.)

Deacon:	(Chung is also shaking) "Listen, Greg, you want me to tell your daddy what kind of naughty, sinful boy you are? Get off now!"
Greg:	"I...I..."
Deacon:	"So do it, why don't you? See—you're just a little chickenshit queer. You think I don't know what's going on upstairs?" Greg suddenly takes his pen and raises it above his head.
Chung:	(Grabs Greg's wrist with the pen) "Greg, what do you have in your hand?"
Greg:	(trembling, tears in his eyes) "The electric hand drill."
Chung:	"OK, kid, you're doing fine. Now do it in slow motion and try to hang-on to what you're feeling right now."
Greg:	"I can't, I can't! I'm blanking out."
Chung:	"No, Greg, you're not blanking out. It's OK, I'm still here. Do it, Greg."
Greg:	(closes his eyes and places the "pen" on my forehead).
Chung:	"Scream your feelings out, Greg! For Chrissake,!"
Greg:	(lets out a horrid scream and everyone backs off, even the young male attendant.) "I hate you! I hate you! I'll kill you, you S.O.B!" (Greg grinds his teeth, growls, and screams "fuck" many times.)
Chung:	(still holding Greg's wrist with the pen on Deacon's forehead) "Who am I, Greg? Who are you killing?

Greg's eyes are closed and he is still shaking all over. I feel wetness on my stomach where he is sitting. I push Greg off and take the pen away. I shake him vigorously, yet my voice is soft, whispering, and gentle.

Chung:	(continuing softly) "Greg, just say it. Who are you angry with? Somebody upstairs molested and beat you? It's OK."

Greg: (soft trembling whisper) "My dad. He did it. And I killed him."

I had everyone circle Greg as I hugged and held him tightly. The others were all crying. Big, grown-up psychotic murderers and rapists crying! Even the male attendant and I cried.

Later, I read Gregory's file. At the time of the homicide, he was all over the front page of the major newspaper for killing the Deacon with an electric hand-drill. There were sixteen drill holes in the victim's head and face. Greg went to trial and was sentenced to life as a criminally insane juvenile. All the files and news articles reported that Greg had been sexually molested and regularly beaten only by the Deacon. The psychodrama proved an inner truth that was otherwise, but no one would listen to me. I was considered just another idealistic greenhorn intern.

After six months of individual and group sessions my recommendation for Gregory's transfer from the criminally insane to the general population of the institution was accepted. I then persuaded the neurology group to train Gregory as an EEG assistant technician. He became one of the best EEG assistant technicians they had ever had.

Loss of an in-house skirmish for a large National Institute of Mental Health grant finally resulted in my happy return, with my family, to the brighter climes of California.

However, before leaving, some of the patients in the schizophrenic ward (who had been placed in the kitchen as part of their rehab) baked a huge three-layer cake for my going away party. This was done with the assistance of my first patient, Gregory, and the kitchen chef who I had successfully gotten out of the hospital earlier. It was unheard of in state mental hospitals that patients, whose problem was expressing feelings, would express their gratitude to a staff member who had helped them. I was deeply touched and moved to tears as all the patients marched around me in a big circle cheering and hitting pots and pans.

Psychodrama Theatre: Spiritual Awakening

After many years of working with the severely disturbed, I decided that it was time to embark in a totally different direction. I wanted to work with average "normal" people who were not mentally ill. I wanted to work with normal people to help them understand what hindered their growth towards evolving and becoming spiritual human beings.

I founded and directed the Human Institute psychodrama theatre that had branches in Los Angeles and Palo Alto and was the first to do 40-hour non-stop, no-sleep psychodrama marathons.

I would like to recount one particular psychodrama event that occurred at Pepperdine University during the time I was doing the Human Institute in Los Angeles.

I was in Pepperdine's psychology department, teaching psychodrama and group psychotherapy seminars to psychology and divinity graduate students in their last year. Dr. Holland, who was the chairman of the psychology department at that time, was particularly impressed with my work and had personally attended many of my seminars. He encouraged me to go into private practice by generously offering me a large office space rent-free on the second floor of a building he and his partners owned. In this location, I could also conduct my classes (which had the largest enrollment in the department).

The entire second floor was unoccupied and still under construction, walls unpainted, and concrete floors exposed. It had large floor-to-ceiling plate glass windows facing the top of a church next door. The church had a huge cross on its peaked roof in full view of the office windows.

Normally, I would use colored theatre lights in my psychodrama sessions, but only the regular office fluorescent ceiling lighting was available. I could turn it either on or off for effect.

At that time, I had a few private clients attending weekly psychodrama groups in my Hollywood villa. One of my early private interns in training was a dear friend, Tony Monaco. Tony was a talented play-right and drama and dance coach, working at that time for Hollywood film and theatre studios. He was a most unlikely candidate for any religion and like most actors, was only intent on pursuing fame and fortune in Hollywood. Since I was Tony's therapist and tutor in psychodrama directing, I invited him to attend all my university seminars.

There were only a couple of weeks before the semester ended. Most of the graduates had already signed employment contracts and were about to embark on their first year of work as ministers and counselors. I wanted my graduates to encounter the psychodrama method in such a way that they would never forget their experience.

In-situ psychodrama is an advanced method. If done correctly, it can be very intense and powerful. "In-situ" means "in the here-and-now", an existential approach that attempts to catch participants in total unguarded surprise, like a Zen *koan,* creating instantaneous self-understanding without the student's awareness of the process.

I had altered the traditional method developed by Dr. Jacob L. Moreno to what I have named "Spiritual Psychodrama", which I began introducing in work with individuals, groups, and family sessions, as well as at my Pepperdine classes.

To warm the class up, I began with usual role-playing, by setting up a safe and easy scene that everyone could relate to and be involved in. Then, I informed the class that what followed was to be their final exam, and each was to write an in-depth feedback of their experience to be handed in the following week, at their last class. The scene I had chosen was "The Last Hour of the Crucifixion of Christ—which I made up on the spur of the moment.

Everyone was excited and filled with expectation. Some of the students who had chosen to enroll a second time and therefore knew me, squirmed in fear, leaning back in their chairs as if trying to become invisible. Poor Tony, my private trainee, was unaware of the surprise I had in store for them.

I began by asking for a volunteer for the leading role of the Messiah. Suddenly, the mist of dead silence crept into the room. My heart, picking up the class vibes, skipped a beat and stopped for a couple of seconds. By observing my own responses, I could "read" the spooky and terrified feelings of the stunned students. The smiles vanished, replaced with dread solemnity. No hands went up. Fearing to be selected, everyone went into freeze mode, like stunned rabbits.

I purposely let a minute go by, looking into the eyes of each student, letting my feelings merge into each one, as they squirmed uncomfortably in their hot seats. Like an anesthesiologist prepping a surgical patient, I used the drama of suspense to move the students into the deeper recesses where they lived—that place of unknowing where for most people, fear of the unexpected sleeps.

At this point, dear reader, you are perhaps ready for a peek into my secrets as I work. One of the most complex and mysterious process that occurs when a person is about to enter the first phase of "in-situ" psychodrama, is that he or she suffers as if dying. Only a person who has experienced this breakthrough knows what it is like. Everyone becomes totally involved and feelings fuse as the class awareness becomes one, a phenomenon that usually occurs only after thirty or more hours of a forty-hour psychodrama marathon.

Suddenly, no one is acting—each is being himself or herself, as they are. Everyone is hip to anyone who is still pretending or lying to him or herself. Since Tony was an outsider and a non-believer and also had more training in acting and psychodrama, I selected him. To my surprise, Tony, an accomplished actor and director of his own actor's workshop, was hesitant and a bit shaken like the others.

"C'mon, Tony!" I said, "I thought you were an actor! The script is a simple improvisation."

Tony looked around. "I think a real Christian is better." But no one dared to save poor Tony. He slowly got up and reluctantly walked to the head of the class.

"Chung," said Tony, shaking his head, "you know damn well this is not an easy walk-through part. I'm only gonna do it 'cause I'm paying you hard cash and love you as a friend. But please—go easy, OK?"

Without turning around I replied off-handedly, "No sweat, pal. It'll be over before you can whistle Dixie."

I looked around and asked the class, "All right, I want a couple of thieves and Roman soldiers, one rabbi, and the rest of you as the witnessing crowd—2,000 years ago." Instantly, several volunteered for the parts. The class was facing the large plate glass windows with the church steeple in full view, and a large unpainted wall was behind them.

Before the opening scene, I gave the following instructions to set the mood. "I want everyone to close their eyes or look at the floor. Concentrate on the following. Put yourselves back and feel what it was like living in that time. We are all simple, poor, hardworking people. It is common for such people to attend these public executions, but this day was not your ordinary criminal death sentence. Some of you have known or heard Jesus and become his followers. Some are just simple citizens of Rome who never even heard of this Messiah. Others are just curious."

"We're in a time machine, so let's all go back and put ourselves in that time and place, but as we are now. I want everyone to observe and be aware of their different feelings and states of mind as we enact the scene. Be honest with yourself. Alright, you may open your eyes. As I approach each one of you in the course of this psychodrama, I want you to be spontaneous and say whatever comes to you at that moment. Forget what you have read in the Bible and do not quote famous lines. Speak from your own heart, and in your own words. Let' s begin."

Quickly, I pulled three empty folding chairs to the front of the large windows. I had Tony stand on the middle chair and placed two students standing on the chairs on each side of him as the thieves. I had them stretch and extend their arms as if on the cross with palms up, telling them not to drop their arms no matter how tired. I wanted to simulate pain and discomfort. The rest of the class was to stand as a milling crowd, watching the scene.

The three who were standing on the chairs nearly touched the ceiling with their heads, raising themselves to a good height. Perfect.

I turned the lights off and told the class to turn around and look at the back wall. Everyone turned. They were shocked to vividly see a large and menacing dark shadow of a cross on the wall, superimposed on our three students with their extended arms. The shadows on the back wall seemed as ghosts of the three crucified who had returned to visit this class in the 20th century. I kept the class facing the wall for a while while I primed the two thieves. I asked the first thief, the non-believer to speak.

First Thief: (To Tony) "Ha, ha. Let's see you work your miracle now, if you're the great savior. Yeah, and while you're at it, you can get me off this stinking pole."

Roman Soldier: "Yeah, King of the Jews, call your God—ha, ha."

Second Soldier: "Forget those fuckin' thieves. Let's role dice for the robe of this mad savior..." (The three soldiers squat and shoot craps.)

Chung:	(To Second Thief) "You really regret your crime. You have a wife and two kids at home, crying and starving. You fear for your family and fear what's to come after death. Now, speak to Jesus."
Second Thief:	"What was your crime, friend? I can see you are not a criminal like me. Why are you not afraid like the rest of us? (pause) Can you teach me not to be afraid like yourself?"
Third Soldier:	(To Second Thief) "You shut your stupid mouth or I'll jam this spear up your stupid thieving ass."
All Romans:	Laughing and applauding Third Soldier's remarks.
Tony:	(Raises his head from bowed position, stammering) "Wa. . .wa . . ter. "
Chung:	(Goes down the hall and gets a paper cup of water and gives it to one of the female students.)
First Soldier:	(Jabs a spear into Tony) "Here drink your own blood if you're that thirsty."

(At this point, now that the class was getting immersed into the psychodrama, I made my move. Without the class realizing it, I launched the in-situ psychodrama by having each student act out his real personal feeling as themselves and not acting any parts.)

Chung:	(Suddenly chooses an unsuspecting female student and tells her to give the water to Tony on the cross.) "You are Mary Magdalene. Just touch his lips with your wet hand, then wash his naked feet. Go!"
Mary M:	(Trembling, she goes to Tony and stands on her toes. With her wet hand and she touches Tony's lips. She notices that Tony has shoes on and turns questioning to me.)
Chung:	(Yelling at Mary M.) "Well? Take his shoes and socks off, stupid! Don't you remember he saved your stinking, whoring life? Where's your gratitude?!!"
Mary M.:	(Begins untying Tony's shoes and taking off his socks.)

(Everyone, including the soldiers, are stunned, some backing off, a few putting their heads down, covering their eyes. A few eyes get blurred and red. Most are stiffened by the terrible scene.)

Chung: "Is your name Mary or not? So—do what you feel. Be honest and follow your feelings."

(Both thieves and Tony freeze, arms still stretched, looking down at Mary M.)

Mary M.:   (She takes Tony's shoe off and proceeds to wipe her wet hand on his feet. She leans over and kisses Tony's feet, and dries them with her long hair. Trembling, she suddenly bursts out crying spilling the cup of water on the floor.)

(Tony starts crying, then even the first and second thieves are both crying. Then the entire class joins in unashamed weeping. Even the Roman soldiers lose their roles and are about to cry.)

Chung: (Whispering angrily at the three soldiers) "Don't you guys start balling. Shut-up now! I want you to laugh and ridicule Mary Magdelene."

Soldiers: "Ha, ha… " (weakly) "Hey, whore, you can kiss my ass any time." "Yeah… I am next, baby. Ha, ha."

Chung: (To the Second Thief) "Well—are you ready to die? Do you wish to ask him for some favor?"

Second Thief: (To Tony) "I am afraid to die. I have a family. I admit I am not worthy, but…"

Tony: (Caught off-guard. Wipes *his* eyes.) "I…uh…I mean…Give me your hand." (They reach and hold each other's hands.)

Chung: (Whispers in Tony's ear.) "Tell him something like: say after me, though I walk through the valley of the shadow of death, I shall fear no evil…for our Father who….the Lord's Prayer— you remember?" (Tony nods.)

Tony: (To Second Thief) "Say after me: Though I walk through the valley of the shadow of death, I shall fear no evil... for our Father who art in Heaven, hallowed by thy name..."

Second Thief: (Facing Tony, begins repeating the prayer, really into the character as his own self.) "Though I walk through the valley of the shadow of death..."

(As the two recite the prayers, Chung goes around to each in the class. The prayers can be heard, echoing in the room.)

Chung: (To a male student) "You are just an ordinary peasant. You have never heard or seen any of these men before. Say what you are feeling and thinking now."

First Student: (With difficulty) "I dunno. Kinda numb. Scared. I feel sorry for him in the middle. I don't know him, but I wish I had met him... I mean before this. He comes across very brave and so... I don't how to describe it... I mean, he's dying, and yet it's as if there was somebody invisible he's talking to. It's spooky. It makes me feel.... uh... like I'm guilty too."

Chung: (Whispers to the soldiers, then moves to another female and male student.)

First Soldier: "Hey, let's look around for some of those—what do you call them weirdoes?"

Second Soldier: "Christians?"

First Soldier: "Yeah, let's get us some Christians and kill a few to pass the time."

Third Soldier: "Just when I'm gonna win the robe, eh?"

First Soldier: (Yells to the class "crowd") "Hey, which of you are followers of this man (points to Tony)."

Chung: (Surprising a male student) "You are Peter, his disciple, are you not? Yeah, I think I saw you last week when he was preaching in Nazareth. (To soldiers) Hey, this is one of the disciples!"

Everyone turns to Peter and a soldier walks up to him. "Kill him, kill him!" the soldiers and others yell with Chung.

Student-Peter: "Hey, wait a minute. No way. I never met him in my life. I swear!"

Chung: (To the female student next to Peter) "You must be his wife? Kill her also!" (The female student was actually already so terrified by the whole scene that she grabbed hold of Peter as the soldier tried to pull her off of him.

Peter: (Yelling) "No, no…I mean, yes, she is my wife. Please we are not his followers. Believe me!"

Chung: (Spins around and suddenly grabs an older woman student who has stood stiffly throughout the whole scene, not saying a word and with no visible facial expression.) "I know you are a real believer, right?" (No response). "What are you holding in your hand? A Bible?"

Older woman: (Glancing at the notebook in her arms.) "It's not a Bible, it's only my notebook, see?" (Whispers to Chung) "Pleazzzz, Dr. Chung—don't get me in there! I really am feeling quite sick and nauseous." (Chung releases his grip and walks off.)

Tony & Second Thief: (after finishing the prayer, both were very quiet and appeared humbled by the experience.)

Tony: "Hey, Chung, can I get down now? I'm really drained."

Chung: (Furiously) "What, Jesus Christ? You're not dead yet? What kind of coward are you? You're gonna quit and just walk away from your believers?! You're in excruciating agony and suffering; your blood is practically all over this ground. The poor fellow who pleaded with you is also dying—what do you have to say, your final departing words, from your own mouth, Tony Monaco?"

The entire class stops and turns to Tony standing on the chair. A long silence. Tony looks around, seeing that everyone is watching and waiting for him.

Tony: "My real feelings, huh? (pauses) OK. This is one hell of a mess I'm in. I have a thousand crazy feelings going through me. I'm pissed-off and very depressed... Really sad, terribly sad for everyone, including myself. All the fucked-up bad things I've done to myself all my life. And I see all the same guilt in everyone else, the pain and suffering and stupid locked-up feelings and fears. Looks like I'm gonna have to pay for all the crap in my life. And...and, God, I am scared shitless and don't know what or who to turn to for help—Jesus ..."

Chung: "You are Jesus—so?"

TONY: "Forgive me...forgive everybody...please dear God, *please* have mercy upon our souls and release me...!" (Tony actually let go and openly cried.)

Chung gently pushed everyone around Tony to hug him and hold him tightly. They even helped carry him off the chair. They needed very little encouraging. They rushed up to him. All cried and wept freely and openly without shame. Chung then had the class carry Tony above their heads as if he were dead, walking around the room.

On the wall, the shadow of Tony was raised high as if dead; the procession moved against the superimposed cross. After the group circled a couple of times around the room, Chung took Tony out in the hall and gave him instructions.

I came back into the classroom saying, "All of you have witnessed his death, and now it is the Easter of your life. He returns from the dead. Here he is! Be joyful, for you have been released from your sufferings!"

Tony entered the room, leaping, smiling, and bouncing around like a happy clown, though his eyes were still wet, Chung turned on the lights and had everyone form a circle, and together they all sang *Amazing Grace*.

Chung dismissed the class, saying, "I want all of you to keep this experience to yourselves until you have completed your term paper which is to be feedback of all your feelings in this last psychodrama class. Let the experience sink in, mull it over—alone. Then write and tell it from your heart; let it pour out and don't bother with syntax and punctuation. I want the real truth of how you felt. At least five pages minimum. Good night, sleep well. In the days of next week, before your last class I pray you will all be blessed with revelational dreams. God be with you."

The following week, everyone was present and they all turned in their papers. All were asked to read their papers aloud to the class. The papers were deeply moving and astonishingly revealing of each student's deep feelings. Most were still reeling from their experience. Some went back to re-read the New Testament and reported understanding some passages much more deeply than before. Several commented that they would never forget this class and felt very close with each other, promising to keep in touch. All could not wait to try doing the same with their future clients in the real work world of their churches, clinics, etc.

The student "Peter" was really terrified that he could not stop himself from denying Christ and said that he would have done it again if it really came down to saving himself and his wife. He remarked at the end of his paper that he was quite disturbed that he had taken his religion for granted. He felt he had much more work to do to strengthen his faith.

"Mary Magdalene" like many of the others, read her paper aloud with great difficulty because she couldn't stop sobbing, even as she read to the class. She felt her life had been totally turned around and that she understood much more about the many traumas arising from her childhood abuse. (After being a private client with Chung for a brief period of follow up, she improved rapidly. She later married and had two children.)

The older woman student, around 40ish, covered her paper with tear stains as she wrote it. She mentioned that she had always been the most devoted believer all her life, constantly reading her Bible. But this class utterly jolted her. During the crucifixion enactment, she suddenly realized that she actually felt like one of the witnesses in that time. She was horrified to find herself acting the same way as those who saw Christ die on the cross and did not try to prevent his death or protest to the soldiers. She could not believe she had been so terrified and felt so guilty that she denied that she was a follower, even knowing it was just a make believe re-enactment. She had not wanted to be involved any further with the scene for fear that everyone would see her shameful guilt and lack of courage and faith. She felt just like the hypocrites whom she had severely judged. While reading, her body shook visibly as she desperately tried to hold back her tears.

Without my prodding, the entire class spontaneously grouped around her, hugging her. She let go and wept as she had never done before.

Everyone again joined her and wept. All kept reassuring her that she was not alone and that they too felt as she did.

Tony was not part of the class and therefore had no final paper assignment. His feedback came through phone calls after not sleeping for several days after the class. This experience made him very depressed because he realized that his life had been "shallow and superficial", lacking any kind of spiritual depth. Within days, he made the decision to quit acting and directing—to get out of the whole Hollywood scene altogether. Tony visited me in Los Angeles several years later and told me he had become a born again Christian and a leader and spokesperson for fellow believers. He related many remarkable religious experiences he had gone through after his conversion. He was happy.

Terrorist Plot

I recall one time at my Human Institute psychodrama training school in Palo Alto that I, like everyone else, was terrified when a bomb actually blew out the entire front office. Fortunately, it happened when no one was there on a Sunday. I believe it was God who guided me to cancel the psychodrama marathon workshop scheduled for that weekend.

A few days later, I received an anonymous call from a male, his voice scared and guilty, "Mr. Chung? I hope no one was hurt by that bomb."

Furiously, I demanded, "Who is this? Are you the one who did this?"

"No, it was not me, but I attended a couple of your psychodrama marathon workshops. There were two of us who were secretly sent to spy on you. We were told to report about what you are doing."

"What are you talking about? Who was spying on me and why?" I demanded to know.

"It was just a job, Mr. Chung. I didn't know what was going to happen. I just told them what happened in the marathons. I told them how amazing the experience had been for me, making me really examine and question everything I had always thought and felt."

"So why would someone want to bomb my institute for this?" I demanded.

"When I reported my experience, the person sounded very worried and claimed that you needed to be stopped."

"What?" I continued in disbelief.

"He claimed you were dangerous because your process made people question society values and beliefs of what is American." He said their report would be mailed to me and then abruptly hung up.

A few days later, I received the findings that resulted in that terrorist attack. Of everything ever written about psychodrama, this was the most paranoid. It said that my method was the most threatening of all group process methods. I had to admit my shock and admiration of the precise truth of the report. It described my "dangerous genius" in "zapping" and my unfailing "zero-targeting" by intuitive "dowsing" for the person's basic unconscious conditionings, and then locating the hidden "spiritual black hole". In short, my psychodrama theatre was believed to be a serious threat to the American way of life. A few weeks later, one of my Stanford political science students showed me the same report written by an anonymous author appearing in the extreme right-wing newsletter of the John Birch Society.

On Tour with Bapak

Bapak was given the royal treatment whenever he visited a city where many people practiced the latihan or wished to be opened to it. The membership usually went into a golden hurricane spin of mad activity, finding accommodations in private homes and hotels for Bapak's entire entourage, plus a large enough hall for his talks every other night. The women went shopping, cooking, selecting clothes, finding babysitters, and arranging transport.

During these visits he often demonstrated latihan testing. We were all blown away as we witnessed Bapak, tall and serene, demonstrating his receiving to test questions. After one question, he explained that even our voices and the sounds we make need to undergo purification until the words and songs of our worship are moved by God's power. He urged us to be patient, that in time we would experience personal revelations in accordance with our development and needs.

Every religion that was sent down contained a different message, since mankind's needs differed for each era. He went on, "I shall ask and myself receive how the prophets of the past worshipped."

He stood up and sang as the Prophet Abraham. You could smell the dry, arid desert, and hear the lonely, eerie wailing of Prophet Abraham's pleading voice.

He followed with the Prophet Moses. Bapak's large chest expanded in front of my eyes, his head pointed straight up, and his voice came like large boulders thundering into the room with the majestic authority of Divine command. Like the other men present, my eyes rolled back, and my head was pushed backwards by the powerful force of Moses's deep bass voice, shaking the room with its booming vibration.

After a brief pause, he stepped forward receiving the way of worship of Jesus Christ. With both arms raised upwards, a high tenor voice gently caressed my brow. My heart wept in gratitude for unexpected forgiveness, as one of Bapak's hands came down in a blessing. Everyone's head bowed and with our hands clasped together, men wept. We were all transported back two thousand years—you could feel the enormous suffering of those days. My heart could not take in anymore, I gasped for air, and my face flushed hot, my legs numb and weary.

Finally, feeling the worship of the Prophet Muhammad, he slowly went down on his knees and in total prostration, his voice emitted, "Allahu Akbar... Ashadu al-la ilaha illallah". I could feel the hot wind blowing on the expansive desert. Never had I experienced such depth of sincerity as in Prophet Muhammad's devout worship.

Then Bapak suggested we take a break, go out, maybe take a short walk in the San Francisco night. It was near dawn and the fog was rolling in. The night-smells of the Middle East were still all around us. No one felt like speaking; each of us was still trying to catch his breath. We returned shortly, and Bapak continued speaking to us until sunrise.

Upon hearing what happened that night, many more people filled the room on following nights. We had felt precisely how the messages of the different Prophets were each custom-tailored to its era and adjusted to the culture of the times. This latihan clearly comprehended all the Prophets.

With Ibu in Golden Gate Park

That memorable summer in San Francisco, I was lucky to drive Bapak and his wife Ibu in my old station wagon through San Francisco's Golden Gate Park, only to be betrayed by my radiator. Ibu remarked, "Look, smoke and water on window—car in trouble, yah?"

Pretending to remain cool, I tried to calm Ibu down by turning on the windshield wipers and replied, "No problem, Ibu, this is San Francisco's morning foggy dew." Bapak knew better and laughed at my futile attempt to con his wife. Suddenly, the radiator exploded and shot its hot water up like Old Faithful.

Giggling like a dove, Ibu patted my manic-depressed shoulder, "See, now you all hot steam mad, you good funny Chinaman," her laughter rang like silvery chimes, detaching me instantly from my car crisis, and everyone joined in the laughter. Cool Ibu mimicked my California lingo, "No plablum, yah?" No wonder the women always stayed close to her. I wouldn't have minded curling up on her lap too.

Vancouver, Canada

Two or three years later, I was in Vancouver to join Bapak during his visit there. When we came out of the latihan, I followed Bapak downstairs. One of Bapak's original companions, Mas Prio, was there. The crowd was still upstairs doing the latihan. I sat down outside of a pharmacy on a bench and Bapak sat next to me. Prio said, "Sam-Tio, you stay here with Bapak. I want to go into this pharmacy."

While he was gone, Bapak and I saw the crowd coming down from upstairs. I had never seen it from his point of view because I was always in that crowd before. Their eyes were big, their cheeks were glowing, just like little children. Each was open, wide-open; I could feel them all coming down like a crowd of children as if coming out of a museum, or a Disney picture, and they were all staring at Bapak—delighted.

I could feel Bapak's body get closer and closer, until his thigh hit right against mine. It felt as though my hip was burning. I thought he was doing that purposely to heal my legs. It was like a heat flash that went through my whole body. I felt my back getting straight, my hips got solid. It felt like I was on a cushion, though it was actually hard marble. It felt like I was floating; my back was straight and my head was so clear. It was like the first time on a mountain—the feeling the snow and the crispy air gives. My ears felt like big holes that the air blew through. It seemed so crystal clear.

Before I knew it, these people were not looking at Bapak, they were looking at *me*, next to Bapak. They looked at me and asked me these questions that were really meant for Bapak. I could feel him talking through me. So my mouth opened and I talked and answered everything. I didn't understand Indonesian, but he wasn't saying anything. I could see from the periphery of my eyes that he was just smiling, looking around.

I saw Prio looking through the magazines, looking at the prescription counter and picking up a couple of bottles of coke, and what-not. I thought, *"When are you ever gonna come out, Prio?"*

As he dodged between the aisles, every now and then he'd look at me and smile, like, "Okay. Continue."

This crowd was just all over the place. Before they even asked a question, I'd give some cockamamie answer. I was playing, I was having fun and enjoying it immensely. I could feel the questions coming and I had the answers ready before the question even hit my ears. It was just amazing. I thought, *"oh, wow! It's like magic."* I was like a kid, delighted with a new magical toy!

It wasn't as if I thought, oh boy, I'm a prophet or I'm like the disciple Paul, or anything like that. No, I was like a kid and I realized that I was actually a puppet with its strings being pulled. And I knew I had to remember it. *Remember this. This is the way Sam-Tio is. Stay with this. Don't let it go. This is what Sam-Tio is. So back off, Tien-Yau. Stay the way you are. You see how it feels. You're clear now about Sam-Tio, your twin soul brother. Dance with it. Accept it. Don't question it."*

Finally Prio came out and took hold of me while Bapak took hold of me from the other side, and boom, I was with them and off we went. I stayed with Bapak, even when he went into his suite. Prio said "Wanna Coke?"

I said, "Whew, yeah, I could use a Coke."

It was Bapak who poured me a coke, smiling, "Yah." He seemed pleased.

I mean had he had known all this time. He had recognized it already. What more confirmation did I need? Tien-Yau was this simple idiot who required scientific proof or something. Let him go.

A Talk from the Pool Table

I went to Indonesia in '67 to attend the first national Subud Indonesia Congress. Bapak personally accompanied me and assigned me to a special room directly across from the famous "Sigmund Freud" of Subud, Mas Sudarto. I later learned that this area was nicknamed "Crisis Alley". Personally, I would've denied that I was in a crisis, because I not only had vivid recall of everything, but I could actually tell you what others were feeling and thinking.

Across from my room, there was an Indonesian guest and we got along marvelously even though I thought he really *was* a crisis case, totally "amok" (one of the few contributions of the Indonesian language to English, meaning literally, suddenly running wild). We both felt we were never out of a "receiving" state, which is perhaps why we felt bonded. Bapak had assigned men helpers to take turns watching him, but he would slip off without notice, only to be found later sitting on a branch of a nearby mango tree, completely naked at midday. Later, I saw this same man but barely recognized him. He was a very pleasant and respectable-looking local attorney in a handsome suit.

Sudarto's place became my second home. I was treated as if I were "Darto's brother", without judgment, totally accepted by his wife and ten children.

One night, Pak Darto leaned over with his large teeth and keen eyes looming, and whispered to me to be at the poolroom next to the latihan hall after midnight if I liked surprises.

A little past midnight, there were less than a dozen men in the poolroom, but this number quickly increased as word got around. We were quietly watching Haryono, Bapak's son, and Mas Adji, his grandson, shoot a game of pool.

Suddenly, all the men went quiet and the pool game stopped. I had often wondered what Bapak was like in his own hometown. I quickly discovered.

Bapak stepped in as if he happened to be taking his usual nightly stroll in the steaming hot, humid Java night. His wrestler's chest bulged from under his shirt. He was wearing loose grey slacks and old slip-on shoes minus socks. I now saw the soft, warm, simple, and charmingly captivating "ordinary persona-without-ego". Everyone stood up and bowed, but he waved for us to remain seated as we were, "Yah, yah".

On many of the following nights, Bapak gave these impromptu men-only poolroom talks with testing. Later he gave women-only talks on Sunday mornings. When he got them laughing uproariously, you could hear the squeals across the whole small village.

For the men, sex was often the subject. Men, Bapak would laugh, are basically impotent spiritually and still hung up having sex with their minds and desires—instead of with the sex organs of their human soul, which hopefully would develop in time (I wanted to know when!).

He demonstrated by testing how Bapak's voice was like now, how it had been at forty, thirty, and twenty. Bapak's voice at sixty-seven was like Moses, a deep, powerful baritone that created an earthquake in my stomach. Then at forty, it was thundering with high energy and I could hear an awesome roaring tiger. At thirty, his voice made me feel like a soaring eagle dancing with his eagle mate. And at twenty, Bapak's song felt like a handsome prince asking God for a wife.

He stopped then and remarked, "If Bapak continues, all the women here and for miles around will get too excited, so Bapak best stop". He laughed. The next morning, many of us noticed that our wives seemed very alive with rosy cheeks. Later the next day, I went to the latihan hall alone. I tried to sing like Bapak. When I asked my wife afterwards if she had felt anything strange, she said, "Nothing, except wondering when and if you're coming home for dinner." Well, I figured her soul needed to develop more and I should be more patient. I really believed this, and yet I also knew better. I could feel the *yin* and *yang* of myself, the lies and truths side by side.

Bapak also tested how each of the Prophets Abraham, Moses, Jesus Christ, and Muhammad spontaneously acted in life. All were in constant crisis being so near to Almighty God, and by today's standards, they would be either arrested or placed in an institution for the insane. It was good warning for us to be cautious in doing the latihan in public unless we wished to be put away. Well, I thought, they couldn't put me away because I had started working as an intern-psychologist in the asylum after doing the latihan for a year. I was more looney-tuned than the inmates even then. Bapak reminded us that we should not fear crisis if it is sent by God. Bapak's own spiritual crisis had lasted one thousand days and nights (he let out a belly laugh as he said this).

I can't remember most of his stories because I was too stoned just breathing his incredible perfumed "fragrance". I remembered my first latihan with Bapak in San Francisco when I held on to his shoe, inhaling this same "fragrance" and I thought I was in heaven. I had asked Sudarto, where could I buy the shaving cologne Bapak uses. Laughing, he replied, "Not for sale—only God gives such fragrance to special people".

Remembering….

Bapak half sat on the pool table, his slippers off, and his hand casually caressed his tired feet. Strange, I was six feet away and I could actually feel my feet being tickled as Bapak scratched his. He turned and looked my way. He flashed his famous whimsical smile, the laser smile that always lifted my soul off the ground and made me feel the urge to run far from my crawling, earthbound sins.

Like waiting for the jet to take off, the wheels slowly move, the jet noise now deafening, my seat shakes like a nervous race horse just before the gates fly open. Automatically, my hands double-check, pulling my seat belt tighter.

…mouth is dry and hand reaches and grabs hold tightly to the armrest as my heart jumps up into my throat. Suddenly, kaaah…ZooOOM, I'm being lifted off a thousand, two thousand, ten thousand feet, my body pressed back by the G-force of his voice, and as the earth tilts, my brain falls off, breathing stops in mid-air.

My soul is soaring way beyond my feelings. Everything feels light and expansive as my understanding spreads its wings wider and wider, taking in greater revelations. My mind is flying right through the second, third, fourth, and right smack into the fifth dimension, on the world's fastest spiritual aircraft, heading towards the Throne of God. I weep unashamedly, my heart blasted wide open, the sins of my ancestors, like leeches on my back, falling off, screaming.

I can hear my voice, "Allah, Allah, forgive me, please…" In the distance I hear Bapak's voice, "Yah, yah, yah". Then I feel Prio Hartono's hand soothing my back. Bapak turns, smiles, and nods to Prio, who nods back that all's well with this Chinese soul who is mumbling "Allah, Allah, Allah" on his knees in that hot humid mystic Java night.

Others that night also moaned, wept, bowed, or lifted their heads with dripping sweat. No one even tried to pay attention to the others. Each was experiencing his own inner cosmic journey. Now I was not alone. All the men began tripping off into their own spiritual hyperspace. Before long, the whole room seemed to float upward to the ceiling. And Bapak simply smiled, laughed, and teased us, "What? You wish Bapak to continue? It's already after 3 am!" And everyone nodded "Yes, yah, yah!"

As he continued talking, his hands kept rubbing his bare feet and I could feel my whole body being massaged, and my chest swelled so wide I was afraid my head was going to fall into its gaping hole. I noticed the other men also had their eyes half-closed, their bodies rocking and swaying back and forth automatically. If their eyes could not look directly at Bapak, they spontaneously lowered as before a royal king.

Bapak's giant soul grew larger than the sun as he continued until 6 am, raining down immense gems of understanding. The light of this dawn then rested its wings on the pool table next to Bapak.

Everyone's cup was filled to overflowing with sparkling diamonds and pearls of wisdom all over the poolroom. Out the door, the golden light shown and radiated, turning every man's soul into the most beautiful, handsome, princely knight, each of us proudly holding his banner and vowing that we shall never let the flag of this latihan fall. Each of us understood that as we march forward, no matter how great the resistance, our surrender to God must be even greater.

Bapak smiled, seeing all our eyes closed. Is this what the Prophets saw, confronting their followers upon descending from each one's own Mt. Sinai? Bapak rose and bid us good morning, "Selamat pagi", and we all chorused back, "Selamat pagi, Bapak. Terima kasih (thank you)."

That incredible evening was followed with other talks each of the following nights. And as the word spread, more men came to hear these midnight poolroom talks.

Later, another truth of our experiences hit home—that this was not another crazy spiritual cult with a quack guru leader doing magic until all of us were in his charismatic spell. When each of us went back home or to work or to be with our parents and old friends, they too became infected to some degree. This great life force that each of us carried touched others.

Since this incredible visit to Bapak's home, and subsequent visits, and on for the next fifty years, I have continued with this method of approaching God. My latihan always begins by first being quiet and then spontaneously letting go, surrendering all and everything, permitting God to move me and do whatever He wills with me, without using my mind, will, or desire to interfere in any way. My Muslim name, Husain, is the name Bapak gave me in recognition of my devotion to surrender-without-ceasing, inwardly and outwardly, to the One God.

My soul's path was to become a psychodramatist. I worked with many, many people—in prisons, hospitals, clinics, higher education, and with thousands who attended my psychodrama workshops. Many became Subud members (as Bapak predicted back at the beginning) and many others experienced a newly awakened connection to God within the religious tradition of their birth or other chosen religion.

My work with people was as a catalyst for each person to uncover what was blocking the emergence of their own identical twin, their soul, their authentic self, and for each person to live more fully and authentically—to find God the therapist that is contained within the soul of each human being.

Epilogue

For years I felt cursed for having been born a cripple. As a child, I remember fuming with rage that I couldn't run and play like the other kids. Why? Was it fair that I was like this? I recall having once fantasized if I should meet God, I would ask him: *"God, why did you create me a cripple? Are you punishing me? What did I do wrong?"* Had I been born normal, I probably would not have embarked on my quest—as if searching for some missing piece in my self to make me whole and complete. In time, I came to understand that my handicap was God's secret gift and that pain and suffering were the basic fundamental passage I experienced in the process of real human spiritual change.

In my searching for God, I was actually searching for my soul. I came across a spiritual path that was not a teaching. It was not an idea or even belief in God, it was a personal intimate relationship, a powerful direct reality experience with His power or force. This was a spiritual *worship process*. The latihan entered, touched, and awakened the sleeping dragon within me—the painful childhood traumas, bottled up anger, emotional hang-ups, the old wounds, and dark terrors. I had to face all my insecurities, self-hates, rage, arrogance, and a host of faults and unspoken transgressions. All of this made up Tien-Yau whose faults were the barrier to the arising of his human soul, Sam-Tio. This is what I went through and out of this I got to face my true soul. I found my identical twin.

My healing art came about because of my life experience. I wanted to put people through a process so that they could find their own human soul. In psychodrama I *became* the sleeping dragon that kept their inner treasure, their soul, hidden. I personified the barriers that they put up that prevented them from experiencing their soul.

The closest I can describe the art of my healing is a prayer in action. If the wish to change was genuinely sincere, then miracles inevitably happened. I saw again and again that the leap of courage and faith and the acceptance of the pain and suffering to face vicious dragons ultimately created an expansive freedom and opening of the heart to receive the awakening power of the great life force of creation. True healing is the healing of the human spirit. When someone finds this, they are experiencing his/her own religion. The true religious process is the action of the human soul.

Now I understand why the disciples didn't write—it is impossible to write in the midst of such an experience. Likewise it is very difficult for people undergoing a therapeutic process to attempt to write simultaneously and coherently about their experiences. It has taken me fifty years before I was able to write this book. I hope you've enjoyed this story a fraction as much as I've enjoyed living it.

Appendix

My style of psychodrama was not the classical Moreno role-playing about family of origin. Here are a couple of examples of the kind of psychodramas I did.

The Stutterer

One Sunday morning, I happened to drive by the furniture store that was closed. I noticed there was a brand new, beautiful blue upholstered swivel chair next to the dumpster. It had one bum leg—like me. I tried to lift it into my van, but the chair was too heavy and awkward.

I looked up and across the street I saw a guy with a large backpack with a blanket roll walking alone.

I loudly called to him, "Hi! Sir? Can you give me a hand with this chair?" He turned and came across the street. He looked at the chair and without saying a word he picked it up and loaded it into the van. Just like that.

I reached out my hand to shake his.

"Thanks, fella. My name's Husain—and you're?"

"I'm...ah...mm...uh, my name's Jay...J.L Lewis," he stammered nodding his head.

I slowly responded, "I really appreciate your help." I reached for my wallet and gave him a five-dollar bill. "Thanks a lot. Oh, by the way, did you just arrive in town?" He nodded. I continued, "If you don't mind me asking, do you have or need a place to stay?"

A big grin crossed his face as he nodded his thanks for the tip. Instantly, I felt he was a good man, one I could trust.

"I'm in the process of moving, and I could use some help. I can offer you a couple of nights lodging and food for your help," I said.

Again, that big grin came on, like the innocent country bumpkins I had known on the Midwest farms.

We drove off. J.L. was in his early sixties, and stood at least six foot tall, with light brown thinning hair, slim with broad shoulders and big, strong calloused hands. I strongly suspected he was from a farm.

When we got to my house, I offered him a cup of coffee.

I asked him, "If you don't mind my asking, have you ever been helped with your speech problem?"

"You mean mmm . . . my stuttering?" he pointed to his mouth. "I'm used to it af....af...ter all the...these years."

I responded, "I realize it doesn't bother you, but are you aware it does affect others. Like, when we first met and I noticed it, automatically I began to speak slower and more clearly. You didn't know that, huh?"

He shook his head in surprise. I nodded and asked him, "If you would like, I can try to help you to stop stuttering. At no charge, of course."

He was delighted, "For real? Sure thing, I...I'm game."

"First, let me ask you a few questions—like when did it first happen and what was going on just before you began to stutter."

For the next half an hour this is the story he related. He was only a year old when his parents died in an auto accident. He was adopted by his foster parents. His best and only friend since childhood was Bobby.

When Bobby turned 19 years old J.L. was 16. "I wor ...worshipped Bobby and he bought a car, a b..b..brand new shinning red Chevy Camero."

They both had gone for a drive. They stopped and bought two cans of beer and continued driving as it turned dark. The beer had made him relaxed and a bit sleepy. He fell asleep as Bobby continued driving with the radio on.

When he woke up in the hospital from his two days in a coma, he was told that he was in a terrible auto accident that killed his friend. He survived without a broken bone except for a few cuts and bruises.

Bobby's parents came to his hospital room very upset and angry. Bobby's mom screamed angrily at him, "You killed our son—you should've been dead instead of Bobby."

When J.L. was discharged from the hospital, he went directly to Bobby's parents home. He rang the doorbell.

Bobby's mom opened the front door shocked, "How dare you come here!"

J.L. nervously holding his cap in his hands, replied, "I…I ca…I came t…to say I…I'mmm…sorry. I..I..mmm to b..b..blame for Bo..bby dying."

She screamed at J.L, "I don't ever want to see you again!" She slammed the door.

For over a month he did not speak, and when he finally did, he began stuttering. His stuttering had continued to this day at 66 years old.

"OK, we're going to do a make believe," I moved two chairs side by side, "I'm going to be Bobby driving and you're sound asleep riding in the car. Now close your eyes."

A bit nervously, he shut his eyes.

Without disturbing him I laid down on the floor next to his chair. Suddenly, I grabbed his left foot tightly, screaming and violently shaking his leg, "J.L.! J.L.! Wake up—hurry, get some help! We just got in an accident, and I'm hurt real bad!"

J.L. opened his eyes in terror with me lying on the floor. He jumped up but couldn't move because I held his foot tightly. "I can't, I can't, Bobby, my foot's stuck!"

I started shaking, trembling and gasping for air as if I'm having a heart attack, "Why, why did you fall asleep! You should've woken me up—I was dozing and didn't see that other car."

I let my head fall, closed my eyes and mumbled, "It's your fault, you fell asleep…all your fault…you can't even get help." As Bobby, I pretended I had just died. J.L. fell down on his knees and held my head. He kept shaking his head, unable to say a word.

I got off the floor and went behind him as he remained on his knees. I put both my hands on his shoulder, and softly whispered, "Go ahead and let it go, J.L. Your best friend just died. Just let all your feelings out—it's OK"

Still on his knees J.L.'s shoulders started to shake, his head went down into his palms, lips trembling and a soft scream issued forth as his whole body shook, crying softly, barely audible.

Very gently I raised his head and guided his body to lay on his back.

After placing two pillows side by side on the floor, I told J.L., "This is Bobby's grave and you're paying your respects. Please lay down. I shall be the spirit voice of your deceased Bobby and I've come to see you.

"Hi, J.L., I miss you and I came to ask you to forgive me for saying those terrible lies—blaming you for that accident. I was scared shitless that I killed you. It was all my fault, I was driving—I should've pulled over when I felt sleepy. And you couldn't get help, 'cause your leg was stuck and then you passed out from your head concussion. You hearing me, J.L.?" As Bobby's spirit I started to sob, pleading that he would come out of his coma, "Please, wake up, brother and please, for God sake, don't blame yourself. You didn't cause me to die—it was me that crashed the car. And I pray you forgive me, J.L. I must beg you to forgive me for blaming you for that accident. It was all my fault, not yours. You did not kill me. Do you *hear me*? Please, please—*Stop blaming yourself! It is not your fault, it is mine!* And please forgive my mom—she's upset. J.L., I can only be free if you really *stop blaming yourself, OK?* I will always love you, J.L., and take care of yourself."

J.L. wept, shaking and lips trembling. After his sobbing subsided, I spoke in a quiet voice, "It's OK now. Don't blame but forgive yourself—this way you will let me go and set me free, J.L."

Slowly, J.L.'s eyes fluttered and opened. Still as Bobby, I bent over and we both hugged each other ever so tightly, and we cried unabashedly.

Before he said a word, I placed my finger on his lips, saying, "Don't speak a word yet, and listen carefully: You must let Bobby go. Whenever you stutter as you speak, you are punishing and blaming yourself by believing that Bobby's death was your fault. You hear me, I'm Bobby now, and you must set me free by not blaming yourself, please J.L., I will always be in your heart."

Only six inches from his face I looked directly into his eyes, and slowly I said, "You will speak slowly—and stop if you're about to stammer. Slowly repeat after me, "Bobby, I will always love you, and I forgive you." I nodded for him to begin.

"Bobby, I will always love you, and I forgive you," he repeated without stammering.

I continued, "I will not punish and blame myself for that accident. I now set you free."

J.L. slowly repeated, "I will n…nah.."

I stopped him with my finger on his lips, and quietly said, "It is alright to stop anytime in the middle, and continue slowly."

He nodded and continued, "I will not punish and blame myself for that accident. I…now set you free, Bobby." His eyes watered and the tears slowly dripped down his innocent country bumpkin face.

After a pause he continued, "…will not blame myself."

I smiled and congratulated him with the thumb up victory sign.

I showed him how to look in the mirror two times daily and speak slowly.

That same day he came up to me smiling proudly. He had called his 26-year-old married son in Okalahoma and for the first time spoke to him without stuttering. His son was overjoyed.

Six months later I got a postcard from him, "Dear Dr. Husain, I thank God and you every day. I'm back home with my son and his family. Now I don't stammer, and I still do those mirror exercises every day. A million thanks, and may God bless you always, Love, J.L.

The Guitar Player/Song Writer

I recall an amazing session in my Hollywood villa Psychodrama Theatre when a young man came because a female friend was concerned that he was depressed and was not speaking to anyone. He had given up playing and composing on his guitar and had actually pawned it. He was very subdued in the marathon. I had my late friend Louis Schumann, who had his guitar, sit next to him. Then I told Schumann to choose a Bach piece and start playing it and then place the guitar neck against the guy's chest but to continue picking. Then I took the guy's left hand and placed it on the frets. I whispered speaking as the voice of the guitar:

I really miss you, master. Nobody has touched me or even looked at me since you left me in this horrible pawn shop. Why can't you take me back home? Can you just caress me a little bit? I miss your touch so much.

I whispered for Schumann to say, "Do you remember that tune you created that went, dum de dum…." while continuing to strum. Suddenly but ever so slowly the guy's fingers started making cords as Schumann strummed the strings. Slowly the guy took the guitar from Schumann and played. Some burst into tears and I had to motion them to weep quietly. For the next ten minutes he played several of his beautiful compositions. The following week the young man went back to the pawnshop and picked up his old buddy. A couple of months later the young songwriter joined Subud.

About the Marathon Experience

Included with permission from Australian Stanford student participant, Harris (then Peter) Smart, about his experience at Husain Chung's Human Institute psychodrama 40-hour marathon.

Dear Ian,

Hello, hello. Sorry I haven't written for so long, but I hope this letter will make up for it. I really have a lot to tell you. I always seem to be writing letters out of the midst of some frenzy or other. Unload all my shit on my friends. Tonight I'm calm for once, more or less, I think, maybe. Just don't know how I'm going to get down all that's racing around in my mind.

I've been through a tremendous experience since I last wrote to you, maybe the biggest single experience of my life. Has made all these other changes I've been through seem like nothing. All those changes of the summer, just little tremors in the ground, compared to this sudden, violent, earth-shattering explosion. All that drug stuff was to this, something like hand grenades are to hydrogen bomb. I've never been through anything like it, and yet at the same time I feel my whole life has been leading up to it, that I have found the thing I have been desperately searching for, for so many years in so many different places.

And what am I talking about? What is it of which I speak with such enthusiasm? It is psychodrama, the psychodrama marathon, forty hours in a room with forty people, continuous psychodrama under the direction of this man Chung. I've been hearing about it for several months now, strange rumors of this Chinese mad man and his forty hour marathons, picked up hints of this experience which couldn't possibly be conveyed in words, but which was incredibly profound, mysterious and terrifying, an experience after which you would never be the same again. I finally got myself together and went, and it was beyond my wildest expectations.

Where to begin, how to describe it. I don't know, so much happened. My head's exploding. I could go on for a book just about that one marathon, so much of so much intensity was packed in to those forty hours, so many revelations, people going through such enormous changes, so much happened inside me, frenzy of joy, not despair, just too much to say, too much energy in the poor old circuits just aren't used to so much energy they're overloaded. Will try to calm down and organize myself and at least get some of it down.

The key to it all is this man Chung. It's not psychodrama in itself, it's that it's *his* psychodrama that's important. Psychodrama with anyone else would not be the same experience. I never come across anyone like him. Maybe there were a couple of people in Indonesia like him, had his strength, his humanity, had realized themselves to the extent he has, but no-one else I can think of. I just realized I don't really know anything about him. I mean in terms of the facts of his life, where he was born and educated and what he has done and so on, what things he's been through to get to where he's at, to know what he knows. I'm curious of course, but really it doesn't seem to matter. Less than with anyone else I've ever met is his identity in that list of "facts", at any moment he's right there and then out-front who he is, naked. He's Chinese, he must be around thirty-five, forty. He's about five feet two or three, has a game leg. Ironic, because inside, he is the tall, strong, whole man, while all the great hulking people are emotional dwarfs, psychic cripples. He is very strong utterly serene. His psychodrama unleash tremendous explosions of energy in people, years and years of pent-up shit, violence, rage, hatred, bitterness, anguish, come bursting out, the walls run with psychic blood, but he remains unperturbed nothing phases him. He seems to have unlimited energy, he's always *on*, always moving, rapping, devising and directing the psychodrama, acting roles. I found that it wasn't really difficult to stay awake for the forty hours, too much going on for you to sleep, too much energy in the air for you to be able to sleep, but Chung is the only one who is always really *awake*, alert and aware of everything that's happening.

The psychodramas he devices are sheer genius. He talks to someone for ten or fifteen minutes, picks up the crucial facts of their life, who they are, the relationships they're involved in, their hang-ups, their problems, their areas of fear and pain, then sketches the loose framework of a psychodrama, the crucial scenes of a life, the essential line, and takes the person back, has them re-enact the key moments of their life, in order to break the old sick patterns, to literally re-do their life, to liberate themselves from their past. He takes many roles himself and he is a fantastic natural actor. I mean his feelings are instantly and expressively registered on his face and the movements of his body. He played an incredible range of characters, kid brothers, girl friends, he played them all, and then into far, far-out things, like the Leprechaun of Suicide, the Angel of Death.

Again, there is much more I could say. There is all this stuff going round in my head about his being a symbolic, emblematic person, I mean that he seems almost designed on every way to be doing what he is doing in this place, at this time. The ironic symbolism of his mere appearance, and then on into things like he is both American and Chinese, that he brings together both East and West, but all this as yet vague and unformulated and will leave until another time.

Friday midnight.

It's the living room of an ordinary suburban house. There's a stereo set up and a few theatre lights hanging from the ceiling. These are the only props.

There's some carpets spread on the floor in the centre of the room and forty of us sit around them in a circle, smoking, drinking coffee. Already, there's tremendous tension in the air—people's defenses screwed up to the breaking point. Fear and hostility very close to the surface.

Chung comes in with four or five assistants, men and women. They'll take parts in the psychodrama and zap on people and keep things under control. The assistants put everyone even more up tight. They seem hostile, insufferably contemptuous and arrogant.

Chung gives a brief rap. Meals will be served. The bathrooms down the hall. You can sleep, but you must sleep in the room, and don't be surprised if you get woken up. You'll have physical contact, wrestling, slapping, but no punching, kicking, biting, gouging, etc. No drugs, no fucking. If you want to leave, leave now. Once the marathon is under way, nobody can leave until it's over. We're on a ship, going on a voyage out beyond the three mile limit, and nobody can get off.

Everything that happens from then on is spontaneous. Nothing planned beforehand, what will happen at any moment is completely unpredictable. And yet, the thing has a rhythm of its own. Each psychodrama has its own natural organic rhythm.

Psychodramas get initiated in a variety of ways. Sometimes Chung starts them, he picks someone, "what's happening with you?" Starts to probe into them, the necessary scenes of the psychodrama suggest themselves, emerge, are set up. Or Chung will get a circle of people going and out of the inter-reactions in that a psychodrama will evolve. Some people just crack spontaneously, their rage, fear, pain get too much, and they are catapulted into their psychodrama. The end of one psychodrama will bring other people crashing down with it and another psychodrama will explode directly out of the last. A conflict between two people suddenly erupts in a corner of the room and has to be dealt with. A girl suddenly goes into hysterical weeping and is brought into the centre of the circle.

It is all real, more real than "real life", because here you follow whatever it is you really feel to wherever it takes you. Defenses, rationalizations, inhibitions, all shattered. What do you really feel? Act it out to the limit. Go with your feelings to wherever they take you. Not acting in the sense of pretense, affectation, artificiality. Anything smacking of this ruthlessly put down. Acting in the sense of doing, expressing, letting yourself be possessed by your feelings, giving yourself up totally to your feelings. Not what you think, not what wish you felt, but what you feel, what you really feel right now. No matter how dark, ugly, violent, hateful, shameful, it all has to be expressed, to come out, to be purged, for you to get beyond it.

There's no formal structure. Everything's spontaneous. Anyone can come in at any time, as their feelings move them, to act parts, zap, double (to stand behind another and say what he is afraid to express). The psychodramas take many different forms. There are confrontations between husbands and wives, acting out of Oedipal situations. Sometimes it's mostly verbal. Other times people slap, wrestle, embrace. People are buried beneath sleeping bags, symbolizing their psychic death, and must fight their way free. Symbols, fantasies and dreams are acted out. There are fantastic scenes, a lunatic asylum, a saloon in the Wild West, drunks at the bar, a women/men strip night club— anything to get people to the breakthrough place in themselves, to get them out of themselves.

But for all the apparent anarchy, there is a definite rhythm. Each psychodrama follows essentially the same rhythm. It is a stripping away of psychic layers, and going deeper and deeper into the self. You come in wearing a face, but it is not your real face, this bland mask is not your real face. All the psychodrama, the merciless zapping ("why do you lie?" "why are you so weak, so impotent?" "why are you such a bitch?"), all this is designed to strip away the mask and reveal the real face, the face contorted with hatred and rage, the face with all its marks of weakness and shame. The marathon is a true mirror and for once, you must look at your real face. The marathon pushes you right up against the walls of the prison you've built for yourself. It brings you right against that monster in you, that dragon you've never dared to battle with. It takes you into that secret place in yourself, that ultimate fear or shame, that place you cannot confront, but *must* confront if you are ever to be whole, to be free.

And of course, this involves much terror, panic, and anguish. You don't want to look at that face. You run shrieking from it. The psychodrama brings on a terrible crisis, an agony of self-knowledge. There were times when I look around that room and it was like some circle from Dante's

Inferno, everyone in Hell, walls running with blood. Curses, tears, screams of rage and pain, people howling and clawing at each other. But what you find is that you can always get beyond that place, the dragon can be overcome. That on the other side, there isn't disaster, disintegration, madness, loss of self, but rather underneath that ugly face there is yet another face, your true face, and it is a strong, loving face. After the hell, comes this incredible joy, love and peace. Every psychodrama is this kind of trip into the self, a purgation, a cleansing, a trip through your hell to realize your true humanity.

40-Hour Non Stop Marathon Advertisement

Husain Chung: Psychodrama Marathon For Madmen Only

This workshop will be a forty-hour marathon beginning Friday midnight and ending Sunday afternoon. It will be a continuous, intensive experience in the acting out of emotions and conflicts. Husain calls his approach "psycho-dramatic karate" because it breaks down intellectualizing defenses and intensifies emotional issues in order to increase one's tolerance for conflict, anxiety and frustration. Rage, anger reduction and interpersonal conflict, may involve participants in physical contact. Ablutions, cleansing and purifications, communal healing tribal rites to exorcise to transform and liberate souls. Meals will be served, catnaps allowed. Bring only sleeping bags. Price of Admittance: Your Mind.

POSTLOGUE: MAGIC THEATER

It is possible that he will one day learn to know himself. He may get hold of our little magic mirror. He may encounter one of the Immortals. He may find his way to a magic theater, the very thing that is needed to free his neglected soul.

Herman Hesse, *Steppenwolf*

About Husain Chung's Psychodrama experience from attendees:

This is soul-stirring work – far beyond role-playing. What I experienced penetrated into my inner being. I left Husain's psychodrama workshop with a sense that I had experienced and been a witness to an ultimate reality that has left me with a sense of wellbeing, peace, and gratitude.

—Lael Belove, *Coach for Life and Human Enterprise*

Psychodrama permitted me to spontaneously explore and release an enormous reservoir of grief which traditional therapy had never achieved.

—Halfrid Nelson Underhill, *Diversified Services consultant:
Nonprofit advancement, Fundraising, Public Relations*

I am deeply indebted to you for founding the organization that gave me tremendous personal healing at a difficult time. My Mystical enlightenment moment experienced at a Human Institute weekend workshop was the pivotal point in my life. Thank you for 'being there' when I needed you the most.....from the bottom of my heart.

—David Fahrland

You were a pivotal catalyst in my journey, without which I likely would have had a very different life trajectory!

—*Julian Spaulding, teacher of Ho'oponopono*

Immediately, like in terms of hours, I was joyous, exuberant, and talkative. Mind was fairly well and enjoyably blown. The intensity of the psychodrama experience was liberating, mind blowing, eye-opening, unique and unforgettable. The trip you are on is so weird, til you see and become aware of the Real You. It is so…it's helping get there.

—*Computer Analyst*

How can one put gratitude into words for the psychodrama experience with Husain Chung? Husain has a unique mix of wisdom, humor, no-nonsense, and an amazing compassionate inner sense to support transformative self-understanding and healing.

—*Stanford Staff Scientist*

For two, three weeks afterwards I felt much stronger, more capable, more able to tolerate being alone, and felt I functioned much better as a therapist and a father. I had terrific energy and little of my usual pessimism. I intellectualized less, simply acted on impulses and spontaneous urges in my personal life and on my job, and was pleased with the results. My clients, colleagues, and friends were astonished and I was not as afraid of the opinions of others.

—*Stanford University Resident in Psychiatry*

I felt washed clean, my sensory apparatus opened, both stimulated and at peace in my psychic plane. I was zipping along the freeway, the top was down, the sun was warm, I had an ice cream cone in my hand, country music singing. I wished the human tribe we had formed did not have to be disbanded.

—*Violinist*

Really spaced out. My entire body was churning and vibrating for several days. I wrote a letter to my father to tell him how I felt about him. He replied in a 12 page letter and among other things said that my letter was the most wonderful and satisfying gift he had ever received.

—*Technical Writer*

I feel the psychodrama Marathon was very helpful to me in a time of greatly felt need. For me most of the changes came in returning to my own environment. The Marathon exploded me
to myself. I could move on from there with a feeling of greater solidity. I learned for certain that to love is a greater test than to fight.

—*Husband, Father with a hot temper*

140

About the Author

Husain Chung worked as a rehabilitation psychologist with the mentally ill, veterans, alcoholics, and prison inmates in addition to counseling individuals, families, teenagers, and couples. He founded the Human Institute psychodrama theatre of which had branches in Los Angeles and Palo Alto. As a member of the Pepperdine department of psychology he taught psychodrama and group process to graduate divinity and psychology students. Husain was an invited group leader in the seminal research study of encounter groups at Stanford University where he was the most highly rated for participant's individual learning, competency as a group leader, and charisma. Husain Chung currently resides in Palo Alto, CA with his partner, Lusijah Rott. He is working on a film project and other writing projects